# The Hiker's Guide
## to **HOT SPRINGS**
### in the Pacific Northwest

*Evie Litton*

## Recreation Guides from Falcon Press

*The Angler's Guide to Montana*
*The Beartooth Fishing Guide*
*The Hiker's Guide to Idaho*
*The Floater's Guide to Colorado*
*The Hiker's Guide to Utah*
*The Hiker's Guide to New Mexico*
*The Hiker's Guide to Arizona*
*The Hiker's Guide to Washington*
*The Hiker's Guide to California*
*The Hiker's Guide to Nevada*
*The Hiker's Guide to Colorado*
*The Hunter's Guide to Montana*
*The Rockhound's Guide to Montana*
*The Hiker's Guide to Montana's Continental Divide Trail*
*Recreation Guide to California's National Forests*

Falcon Press is continually expanding its list of recreational guidebooks using the same general format as this book. All books include detailed descriptions, accurate maps, and all information necessary for enjoyable trips. You can order extra copies of this book and get information and prices for the books listed above by writing Falcon Press, P.O. Box 1718, Helena, MT 59624. Also, please ask for a free copy of our current catalog listing all Falcon Press books.

Cover design by Darrell Pruett
Cover photo by Roger Phillips, Upper Loon Creek Hot Springs,
  Frank Church River of No Return Wilderness, Idaho.
Book photos and maps by Evie Litton.

Library of Congress Catalog Card Number 90-08037

ISBN 0-937959-75-8

# ACKNOWLEDGMENTS

My heartfelt thanks to Ellen, the best friend a would-be writer ever had, who not only allowed me (armed with piles of scribbled notes) to attack her own computer after every trip—but who also spent endless hours trying to teach a strictly no-tech novice the fine art of taming it. Without her help, this project would never have gotten off the ground! I'm grateful to computer-whiz Gerry for solving the jams I got into that were beyond even El's ability to fix. Thanks are also in order for all the honest and helpful feedback I got from Jon, and other friends, who took the time to "play reader".

I'm indebted to the many district rangers of Umpqua, Willamette, and Mt. Hood forests in Oregon, of Olympic National Park, and Mt. Baker-Snoqualmie Forest in Washington, and of Clearwater, Boise, Payette, Sawtooth, and Challis Forests in Idaho—who did their best to supply me with accurate and up-to-date information.

And last but not least, I want to express by gratitude to the friendly folks over at Falcon Press for guiding this stray missile to a safe and happy landing. Without their help, it would probably still be in orbit somewhere over Idaho.

# CONTENTS

## Oregon

## Washington

# Idaho

# INTRODUCTION

Halfway through a peanut butter and carrot sandwich, as I sat on a warm rock gazing up at the Chinese Wall, the sky suddenly turned darker than Slate Creek below. I'd just gulped down the last bite when the drops started to fall, and the drizzle turned to a spitting downpour before I was halfway down the trail. I'd no sooner leaped into the car when the sky turned a sickly shade of yellow and let loose a wild volley of hailstones. The ground, covered with dancing snow peas, turned white in an instant. I slithered the last mile up Slate Creek Road with a smile on my face because the perfect antidote to foul weather was close at hand. While sleet and hail pelted the crude shelter, I was soon waiting out the storm in total comfort—immersed in a cocoon of steamy water.

Being devoted to both hiking and hot springing, experiences like the one above taught me early on that the two go together like cream cheese and lox on a bagel. Whether it's a hot dip sandwiched between strolls or a muscle-melting soak at the end of a rugged trek, the contrast creates a dynamite combination!

I began to comb the backwoods and wildlands of the Pacific Northwest, caught in the clutches of a powerful addiction. Between trips, I'd haunt the library to pour over geothermal maps for hot springs hiding in prime hiking country. As the list lengthened, I felt a growing urge to share it with kindred souls.

And so, the pages of this book began to emerge—often under the most adverse conditions. I'd return to camp and just get all the paperwork spread out on a picnic table when the wind would scatter the lot or a sudden

*Author Evie Litton finds that the bathhouse at Slate Creek Hot Spring offers a fine shelter in foul weather plus a 5-star soak.* Dave Bybee photo.

1

rainstorm turn it to pulp. Often I'd be scribbling away long after dark with the aid of a dim flashlight while trying to dodge the nighttime Kamikaze bugs.

With no space in my tiny car for a laptop computer on top of all the camping gear, an astronomical number of pencils, erasers, and notebooks were consumed in the painstaking process of stringing words together. And I learned that the most grueling hike out there is nothing compared to the effort of capturing it on paper. But at long last the pages are filled (and safely bound), and I leave the final task to you, the reader—to follow the attempts of a first-time writer to share some of her favorite experiences.

# WHAT IT'S ALL ABOUT

"Hot springs? What kind of hot springs?" you wonder skeptically. "Fancy resorts with wall-to-wall bodies packed into chlorinated pools, or just trickles oozing down some slimy bank into algae-coated mud puddles?" Or else, vaguely offended, you mutter, "What's this, hot springs and hikes in one book? Why on earth mix them together—what's the connection?" In either case, you'd like to know what this is all about.

As to the first question, the gems described in these pages aren't the commercial variety. They're located on prime public land within our national forests and parks—where primitive soaking pools are improvised (strictly by volunteer labor) to collect the flow of any spring equipped with roughly the right temperature, output, and location. A hot trickle is no good to anybody without a proper pool to contain it.

Part of the adventure in seeking them out is that you can never be sure what you'll find. One year there might be a rock-lined pool on the bank of some sylvan stream. The next, it may have vanished and been replaced by a different pool, a hand-crafted soaking box, or possibly even a crude bathhouse patched together to shelter users from the elements. If you're the first arrival this season, you may have the fun of devising your own dip.

Streamside pools are subject to washouts during the spring runoff months and by late summer may be left stranded high on the bank—too hot for comfort without cold water for a mix. For off-season use, the ideal spring would be located well above the river's grasp and have either a temperature within the comfort zone or a side stream flowing by that could be diverted.

In the five-star soaks, in addition to other virtues, both the temperature and the flow rate can be manually controlled if need be. This is often accomplished by merely adjusting a rock or two, but sometimes more ingenious methods are called for to channel both hot and cold water from more distant sources. A strong flow keeps the pools constantly (and naturally) cleaned between soaks.

What you're likely to find also depends on the use a particular hot spring gets. The soaking pools located closer to the larger population centers tend to receive more volunteer care as well as more stress, while the condition of those in more remote areas will be more primitive but more pristine as well.

As for the second question (assuming you haven't asked what's a hike): What are hot springs and hikes doing together in one book, and what's the connection? Well, there happen to be several good reasons and an excellent connection.

2

*Streamside pools like this are submerged at high water and must be remodeled every summer. The temperature can be lowered by shifting rocks on the outer edge to let cold water trickle in.*

You've probably gathered by now that it's entirely possible to find soaker-friendly hot pools located in precisely the kinds of places you've always enjoyed hiking: deep river canyons, or misty woods, in the mountains of some beautiful national forest or park—and even a few choice wilderness areas!

Now, doesn't such a delightful treat make as worthy a target for a hike as some peak with a view from the top that you might just have time to catch a quick shot of—if the clouds would move over a bit? Or a remote lake with a finicky fish or two flipping around at the bottom? Well, certainly no crazier, anyway...

OK, so we've established the legitimacy of hot springs as a hiking goal or destination. But not all of these bubblies require a lengthy trek to locate; many lie near the road in some scenic area that offers a choice of intriguing trails nearby. As a prime example, the Sawtooths in Idaho happen to have strategically spaced hot dips close to almost every trailhead.

"So what", you ask. "I came here to climb Mt. Whatzits'name, or to spend a quiet week up at Such'n'such Lake." Fine! But wouldn't it feel great afterwards, back at the trailhead, to ease away all those aches and pains (not to mention the dirt) immersed in a totally natural Jacuzzi shrouded by evergreens? Or, suppose you got yourself drenched and/or frozen up there and are still faced with either a soggy roadside campsite or a miserable drive back home. Yup, you guessed it (you're learning fast)-time for a nice long soak over at Whozit's Hot Springs!

Well, since you're still reading, this offbeat guidebook must be meant for you: the active outdoor hedonist who enjoys experiencing the wonders of nature the hard way—on foot, but who also turns on to the contrasting image of a blissful dip at the end of the trail in one of nature's own steamy creations.

It just so happens that the mountains of the Pacific Northwest are a mecca not only for superb scenery and hiking but also, as it turns out, for first-class primitive hot springs. A chain of these pearls runs right through the Cascades of Oregon and Washington, and in the rugged mountains of central Idaho you'll discover a profusion of precious gems—including eight beauties buried in the River of No Return Wilderness.

The best of both worlds is presented here in one package: a detailed guide to 47 of the finest natural hot dips in these three states, and a trail guide to 53 scenic hikes that either lead to them or begin nearby. Whether you're already a confirmed wilderness buff and hot springs fanatic or new to either pursuit, this book will be a welcome companion to your travels.

# UNDERSTANDING THE DESCRIPTIONS

Hot Springs for Hikers in the Pacific Northwest is a guidebook to both hot soaks and hikes in the states of Oregon, Washington, and Idaho. The springs marked on the three state locator maps are listed numerically. Beneath them in the text, you'll usually find a list of one or more hikes. For example, in Oregon we start with 1. Umpqua Hot Springs, followed by Hikes 1a-c. In

Washington, 7. Olympic Hot Springs is followed by Hikes 7a-c, etc.

The hikes fall into three basic categories: 1) hikes to reach a hot spring, 2) hikes continuing on from the spring, and 3) hikes located in the same area. One or more of the three types may be found listed under each hot spring (or sometimes following two or more springs located close together).

## Headings for Hot Springs

Roadside soaking pools, or those located less than a mile from the road, are not written up as hikes. They normally have just three headings: 1) a general description, 2) directions for getting there, and 3) the hot spring itself.

**General description:** This is a nutshell summary that includes what you'll find there, the distance from the road, the general location, which national forest it's in (so you'll know what map to get), customary swimwear or lack thereof, and elevation (a useful gauge for estimating seasonal access). For example: A quiet soaking pool cloaked in greenery at the end of a .5-mile creekside path, east of Lewiston in Clearwater National Forest. Swimwear optional. Elevation 2,900 feet.

**Directions:** Both the road access and the trail (if any) are included, along with a note as to whether the spring is marked on the forest map. The searcher should always travel equipped with the appropriate forest map; the springs aren't always marked, but the maps are highly useful in finding your way there. Also, the directions often refer to Forest Service roads by number.

**The hot springs:** Last but not least comes a short paragraph or two describing such things as what the soaking pools are like, the temperature and whatever primitive means there may be of controlling it, the general setting and scenery, an idea of how much company you can expect, and how visible the pools are. As a rule of thumb, the swimwear custom (or degree of "skinnydippability") equates with the degree of visibility or distance from the road. A useful formula.

## Headings for Hikes

The hikes are provided with the following headings: 1) a general description, 2) elevation gain and loss, 3) trailhead elevation, 4) the high point, 5) maps, 6) finding the trailhead, and 7) the hike itself. Most of these categories are self-explanatory, but a few additional comments will help you get the most from each hike.

**General description:** This is a brief statement that includes all the basics: the degree of difficulty (easy, moderate, or strenuous), the distance, and whether it's usually a day hike or an overnighter. For example: An easy 5-mile, round-trip day hike to. . . It ends with information about which type of hike it is and where it goes.

For a hike to a hot spring you'll learn what's there, the general location, and the customary swimwear ( . . .to a bubbly soaking box in the Glacier Peak Wilderness, northeast of Everett. No need to pack a swimsuit.) For hikes continuing on from a hot spring or any spot other than a roadside trailhead, the starting point is made clear. For a hike located in the same area, the destination is summarized and the hot spring given for reference.

The degree of difficulty is determined by the steepness of the trail with minor adjustments made for length, short steep pitches, or extreme roughness. A hike is rated as easy if the grade is up to 5%, moderate between 5-10%, and strenuous if the grade is over 10%. You can use the following formula to calculate the grade of any hike: elevation gain divided by 5,280 (gain in miles) divided by length of trail x 100 = percent grade.

**Elevation gain and loss:** These figures indicate the rigors of a hike. The elevation gain is given in one direction only. A round-trip hike that gains 1,000 feet and loses 200 feet on the way in would lose 1,000 feet and gain 200 feet on the way out. This would be written: + 1,000 feet, -200 feet. Or, suppose a hike gains 1,600 feet, loses 400 feet, gains another 800 feet, then loses another 200 feet. The total gain and loss would be +2,400 feet, -600 feet. Only one figure is listed if the hike is virtually all uphill or all downhill.

A loop hike lists just one figure because no matter how many ups and downs there are, the total gain is always the same as the total loss. Consider Hike 11b: the consecutive figures are + 2,800, -280, + 40, -40, + 480, -240, + 120, -120, + 440, -3,200. The total gain is 3,880 feet, and the total loss adds up to the same magical number.

**Trailhead elevation and high point:** These are useful figures to know when trying to determine the access at different times of year. Normally the trailhead is the low point, but sometimes just the opposite is true—as with all the hot springs in the River of No Return Wilderness. In these "upside down" hikes, the headings are changed to make this clear (High point: Trailhead, 8,120 feet. Low point: Kwiskwis Hot Springs, 5,680 feet.) The elevation gain and loss in this case is + 340 feet and -2,780 feet since the hike is nearly all downhill.

**Maps:** This heading lists the USGS topographic quadrangle(s) and Forest Service map(s) for each hike. The USGS quads come in two scales. The 7.5-minute quads are the most detailed; all the newer mapping is being done in this series. They usually have contour intervals of 40 feet, cover areas of about seven by nine miles, and are drawn on a scale of 1:24,000. The more outdated, 15-minute quads usually have contour intervals of 80 or 100 feet, cover areas of about 14 by 17 miles, and are on a scale of 1:62,500.

Topo quads are available at most mountaineering stores or can be ordered directly. To do so, simply list the maps you want in alphabetical order. Indicate how many of each you need, which state they are for, the desired scale, and the price. Standard maps currently cost $2.50 each plus a $1.00 handling fee for orders under $10. Send orders to USGS, Box 25286, Federal Center, Denver, CO 80225. An index of each state's quads is available free upon request.

Libraries at most universities have a complete set of USGS quads as well as helpful staff and a nearby duplicating machine. This makes a dynamite combination—especially when planning one-time trips that wind through three or four quads. The price you pay for such frugality is having to learn a few vital skills—such as how to line up sections of a large map onto a small copier, how to make a sturdy patchwork quilt out of all the pieces you copy, and how to color in with blue (since blue won't reproduce) all the important streams and lakes on your copies.

The Forest Service offers detailed contour maps of most wilderness areas in addition to road maps of the entire forest. They can be bought at ranger stations for $2.00 each and also at many sporting goods stores. A wilderness map (if available) is listed along with the national forest. Although often drawn on a smaller scale with fewer contour intervals than the USGS quads, they tend to be more up-to-date for trail routing and trailhead locations. They feature clearly marked trails and access roads with route numbers. Some even show trail distances between points, but watch out—the figures may be metric.

A trail map may also be found in the text along with each hike. Intended as a general introduction to a given area, these maps should never be substituted for the USGS quads and Forest Service maps recommended. The legend below has a complete list of the symbols used.

**Finding the trailhead:** This heading gives all the nuts and bolts of getting there. Start with the state locator map along with a highway map to get your bearings, then home in on the final access road(s) with the help of the appropriate forest map. (As in the directions to hot springs, frequent reference is made to specific forest roads by number.)

**The hike:** Yes, we finally get to the nitty-gritty, where you'll find out all you wanted to learn about the trip itself, what the route is like, any nasty stream crossings or other obstacles on the way, possible extensions or side trips, campsites, and whatever outrageous viewpoints, delectable hot dips, or other rewards lie waiting at the end of the trail.

# TOUCHING THE LAND LIGHTLY

Most hikers treat the wilderness with care and respect, but some just don't realize they have poor manners. Based on the habits of past generations, they set up camp close to streams and lakes, build fire rings, lean-to's or bough beds, dig ditches around tents, or cut down live trees and brush for firewood. Twenty years ago, such customs may have been OK. Today, they leave unacceptable and long-lasting scars.

While what little wilderness we have left is shrinking before our eyes, the number of hikers grows by leaps and bounds. Thus, a new code of ethics has emerged from the need to cope. The basic rule today is to touch the land as lightly as possible. Observe "no-trace" practices around each campsite, hiking trail, and hot spring. It's our responsibility to preserve the quality of the back-country and its wildlands for future generations.

Choose your campsite thoughtfully and use it lightly. Pick a spot (at least 100 feet from water or trail) where you won't have to clear any vegetation or level a tentsite. Camp on mineral soil, never in meadows or soft grassy areas that compact easily. Leave the area clean and in its natural

# MAP LEGEND

| | | | |
|---|---|---|---|
| U.S. Highway | 🛡️ 00 | River or Creek | 〜➔ |
| State Route | (000) | Lake | ⬭ |
| Forest Road | 0000 | Hot Spring | ● |
| Paved Road | ▰▰▰ | Meadow or Swamp | ⚡ |
| Dirt Road | ==== | Falls or Rapids | ⫯ |
| Trailhead and described trail | ⊝--- | Campground | ▲ |
| Other Trails | ------ | Peak and Elevation | x^{0000} |
| Cross-country Route | ·········· | Glacier | ⬭ |
| Wilderness, Park, or NRA Boundary | ⬅·······➔ | Pass or Saddle | ⫽ |
| Wild River Boundary | —·—·— | Ranger Station | ⚑ |
| | | Bridge | ⋈ |
| Map Scale (miles) | 0  0.5  1 | Building | ▪ |
| | | Lava | ⬭ |
| | | Power Line | ▪-▪-▪ |

8

condition. Make it look as if no one had been there.

The use of backpack stoves conserves firewood. Campfires have been permanently prohibited in many heavily-used areas and in others are banned in summer and fall due to the danger of wildfire. If a fire is allowed (and really needed), dig out the native vegetation and topsoil and set it aside. Don't build a fire ring with rocks. When breaking camp, drown the fire thoroughly, bury the cold ashes, and replace the native soil.

Keep all wash water at least 100 feet from water sources and don't use soap or detergents in or near water. Even biodegradable soaps are a stress on the environment. Clean your cookware with soapless hot water and a bit of sand or gravel—it's often more effective than soaps. If soap must be used, wash in a basin well away from lakes or streams.

Always answer the call of nature well away from any campsites or open water. Dig a hole 6-8 inches deep, bury everything carefully when finished, then cover it with sod or topsoil. If you fish, dispose of entrails by either burying, burning completely, or packing out.

Garbage that can't be burned must be carried out. This includes even the tiny items like gum wrappers and cigarette butts. The plastic-coated foil packages commonly used by packpackers don't really burn and must be packed out as well. Never bury food scraps, because animals will dig them up.

Solitude is an important ingredient of a wilderness visit, so try to minimize your impact on others. Keep noise to a minimum, leave pets at home, and keep groups small. Be courteous in sharing what belongs to everyone, whether it's a camping area, hiking trail, or hot spring.

Cutting across switchbacks on hiking trails (and even walking outside of established trailbeds) can lead to erosion. Try to select routes on hard ground if you hike cross country. If your group must cross a meadow, spread out to avoid trampling a path through vegetation.

Hot springs are as fragile as any other water source and should be treated with the same respect. Soaking pools are precisely that. They're not bathtubs where you can lather up with soap and shampoo. Whatever drains out flows directly into nearby streams, and what can't drain out is there for the next user to find. Also, the damp ground around the springs is often steep and easily eroded, and delicate plant life can be swiftly crushed.

Many of the popular hot springs in Oregon and Washington are already on the endangered species list simply because too many eager visitors haven't learned the basics of backcountry etiquette. At one of these imperiled gems, I was criticized by volunteer caretakers for wanting to share it with the world at large by writing a guidebook. My defense was the sincere hope and belief that you, the educated reader, will treat the hot springs you visit with responsibility and tender loving care.

*This campsite came complete with a kitchen work area and a level slab for the backpack stove (and the cook) to sit on.*

# MAKING IT A SAFE TRIP

Backcountry safety is largely a matter of being well prepared and using common sense. For starters, this means carrying proper survival and first aid equipment, compass, and topographic map—and knowing how to use them. Secondly, tell somebody where you're going and when you plan to return.

Study an area before leaving home, then gather last-minute information from the ranger station nearest your destination. Rangers can tell you about any potential problems or hazards in their area (approaching storms or forest fires, high water, etc.) as well as the current condition of roads, trails, and streams. The office to contact for each hike is listed at the end of the book.

Take along proper equipment. The basics in every hiker's gear should include sturdy but comfortable footwear and warm clothing that will keep its insulating properties when wet, plenty of water (brought from home), extra food, and a dependable tent. You may enjoy beautiful dry weather, but storms can hit at anytime.

Select a hike within the abilities of all in your group and stay together on the trail. If it's getting dark or a storm looks likely, make camp as soon as possible. Never hike at night. Be aware of the dangers of hypothermia and the proper steps to avoid it.

If you get lost, don't panic. Sit down and try to locate landmarks that will help orient you. Check out the topo map and take compass readings. Plot a rational course of action before you move on. And remember, many hikers have spent unplanned nights in the woods and survived.

Don't take a chance: boil or treat all open water used for drinking—no matter how clean it may look. For day hikes, carry a canteen from home with an ample supply. It's a sad fact that wilderness water sources are no longer safe to drink, with the exception of remote springs and fresh snowmelt. Increasing cases of backcountry dysentery, caused by a waterborne parasite called Giardia lamblia, show the impact that water pollution has in the wilds.

Giardia is spread by water contaminated by either animal or human waste. Halazone and chlorine don't work against it, and iodine (besides being dangerous in itself) will kill only 90-95% of all the cysts. Experts say the safest bet is to boil all water; recommendations vary from a minute to 10 or even 20 minutes. There are also a number of filters on the market that are an effective (but expensive and rather slow) means of purifying water.

Don't attempt to ford major streams during the spring runoff. Fast water can easily sweep hikers off their feet—and sometimes to their deaths. In early summer, creeks and rivers can have ten times their average flow in a year of average snowfall. Consult with the district ranger before attempting hikes that involve a ford; when in doubt, wait until midsummer.

Search for a log crossing or for boulders to hop across. Leave your boots on for better traction on the slippery bottom and avoid the current's full force by staying sideways to the flow. Go slowly and deliberately, planting each foot securely. Some hikers carry a sturdy branch for extra support. During the spring runoff or when crossing a glacial stream, the water will be at its lowest level during the morning hours.

Be cautious around hot springs. Some emerge from the ground at temperatures that can boil eggs and would-be bathers alike. Avoid bare feet until you're sure where any hidden hot spots or other hazards are. If a soaking pool feels too hot, don't use it unless you can find a way to lower the temperature. And never mix a prolonged soak with drinking alcohol; it can cause severe stress on the circulatory system.

To prevent problems in bear country, keep all food well wrapped and hang it at night (along with garbage, lotions and soaps) from a strong tree limb at least 12 feet above the ground and at least five feet from the trunk and other branches. Some hikers use two evenly weighted stuffsacks hung by the counterbalance method.

Driving in the backcountry often involves negotiating narrow one-lane roads—some heavily traveled by huge logging trucks and others deserted for hours just when you get stuck. Drive cautiously and exercise common sense. Carry plenty of gas, water, and spare supplies.

*Many hot springs flood the ground with scalding water before reaching a comfortable soaking temperature. The spectacular source of Vulcan Hot Springs is NOT the place for bare feet.*

# HOT SPRINGS IN OREGON

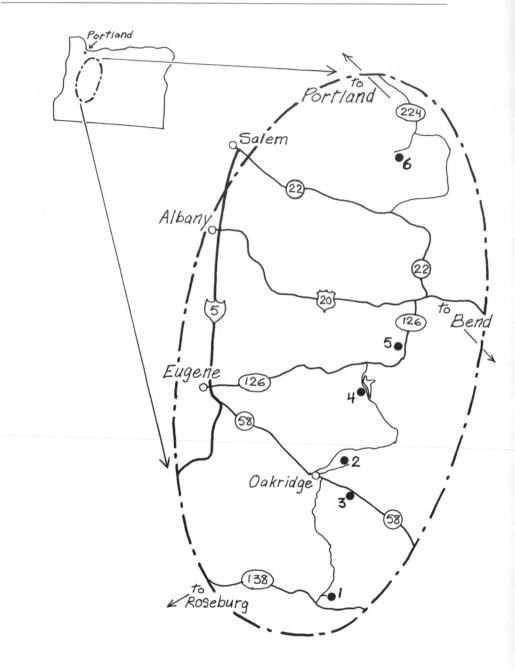

# OREGON

## An Overview

The vulcanism that created the high Cascades also conjured up a number of steaming springs as part of the package. Today's visitor can enter the primeval forests on the west side of the range and discover a chain of inviting soaking pools framed by evergreen boughs. The six gems marked on the Oregon Locator Map are located in national forests with easy access via paved roads and short paths. In addition, all six offer superb hiking on nearby trails that ramble through lush woods to lakes and waterfalls, ancient lava flows, and overlooks of many volcanic cones. Although Oregon has no wilderness hot springs, the hikes listed include a sampling of four of the wildlands now linking the high country in an almost unbroken line.

The tour begins in the south and travels north to eventually continue up through Washington and across into Idaho. Directions are given from major towns along Interstate 5, but it's also entirely feasible to travel directly between dips (see Direct routes, below). In general, the forest roads and hiking trails are well maintained and easy to follow, the campgrounds developed and frequently full, and the bubbly soaking pools often brimming over (at least during the summer months) with other equally eager beavers.

## Hot Springs and Hikes in Oregon

Umpqua Hot Springs and nearby paths in Umpqua National Forest (Hikes 1a-c) are found near State Route 138 between Roseburg and Crater Lake. North of this are Wall Street and McCredie Hot Springs located close to Oakridge and State Route 58 in southern Willamette Forest; nearby trails offer highlights in the Waldo Lake and Diamond Peak wildlands (Hikes 3a,b). Near State Route 126 between Eugene and Bend in northern Willamette Forest come well known Cougar, with a nearby loop in the Three Sisters Wilderness (Hike 4a), and Bigelow, a little known gem below a lush path on the McKenzie River (Hikes 5a,b). Finally, a short stroll leads to Bagby, a unique soaking facility southeast of Portland in Mt. Hood National Forest; a nearby trailhead offers a peek into the Bull of the Woods Wilderness (Hikes 6b,c).

## Direct Routes Between Dips

A combination of primary forest roads and state highways through the Cascades makes it possible to jump right from one hot pool to the next without coming up for air if the reader is so inclined. Read the listings for exact directions and carry the appropriate forest maps. Bear in mind that gas stations and stores are few and far between and that many mountain roads are open only in the summer months.

One forest road, now paved most of the way, links Umpqua Hot Springs with Wall Creek and McCredie. About 47 miles long, it runs north from State Route 138 at Toketee Junction to State Route 58 near Oakridge. It starts out as Forest Road 34 in Umpqua Forest, soon passes the turnoff to Umpqua, then climbs over a 5,000-foot pass into Willamette Forest where it winds up as Forest Road 21.

Another main forest road, this one now fully paved, connects the two hot springs near Oakridge with the two near State Route 126. It covers a 55-mile stretch between State Route 58 at Oakridge and State Route 126 near Blue River—passing the parking area for Cougar en route. (Now that it's paved, old Forest Road 19 has been given a new name: Aufderheide Memorial Drive.) To go from Cougar to Bigelow, drive north to State Route 126 and follow it four miles past Belknap Springs, then left to the river bridge. A total hop of 22 paved miles through Willamette National Forest.

A series of six paved roads will lead you north from Bigelow to Bagby in a grand total of 100 miles. From Bigelow, drive 16 miles north on State Route 126, jog three miles east on U.S. Highway 20, then 31 miles north on State Route 22 to Detroit. Follow signs "to Breitenbush" on Forest Road 46, trading Willamette for Mt. Hood Forest, and go about 41 miles. Hang a left on Forest Road 63 for 3.5 miles, then a right for the final six miles on Forest Road 70, signed "to Bagby Hot Springs".

### Season

The hiking season in the moisture-laden Cascades ranges from year around for the low elevation hikes near Umpqua and Bigelow Hot Springs to summer months only for the higher routes in the vicinity of Cougar, McCredie, and Bagby—where snow often obscures the trails from October through June. Summer weather on the west side of the crest can vary from bright sunshine to damp rainclouds, sometimes in a matter of minutes—so it's best to travel prepared for the worst.

# 1 Umpqua Hot Springs

**General description:** A grand old soaking pool on a short new path, overlooking a wooded canyon in Umpqua National Forest, east of Roseburg. Keep swimwear handy. Elevation 2,640 feet.

**Background:** Umpqua has a history of challenging approach routes. Some years ago, the hopeful hot springer had a difficult choice to make. A round-about jeep track followed by a primitive path snaked down the far bank of the river from "the Meadows". The alternative was a muddy slide downhill to do a tightrope act across it on a slippery log. Then, just a few years back, the Forest Service built the hazard-free North Umpqua Trail along the far bank. This route provided not only a cool walk through a quiet forest but also a comfortably uneventful access.

Nowadays, a sturdy bridge built in 1987 spans the North Umpqua and offers the ultimate approach to the soaking pool. It leads to a .25-mile path joining the last segment of the North Umpqua Trail (Hike 1a). No more jeep roads, muddy banks, or slippery logs to bar your way but help ensure your privacy at this once secluded spot. Be prepared to wait your turn for a soak—especially on summer weekends.

**Directions:** From Roseburg, drive east on State Route 138 about 60 miles to Toketee Junction and turn left on paved Toketee Rigdon Road (Forest Road 34). At the bottom of the hill, bear left at the "Y" and drive past Toketee Lake and Campground. Turn right at 2.3 miles onto graded Thorn Prairie Road

*The shelter at Umpqua Hot Springs faces a broad view over the North Umpqua Canyon.*

(Forest Road 3401) and drive 2 miles to the parking area. The path crosses the new bridge and soon joins the North Umpqua Trail to climb the steep riverbank. A few more dips and rises east and you'll emerge from the woods to spot a 3-sided shelter on the edge of a bluff.

**The hot springs:** Sculpted from colorful travertine deposits, a pool measuring about 4 by 5 feet perches on a bare cliff 150 feet above the North Umpqua River; the tree-flowing curves make a uniquely attractive container for the 106-degree water trickling through it. Shaded from the elements within a 3-sided, shingle roofed shelter, a sun deck on the open side provides a pleasing view over the canyon below.

---

# HIKE 1a *Umpqua Hot Springs via North Umpqua Trail*

**General description:** An easy 3.6-mile, round-trip walk to the hot springs on a wooded path near the route described above.
**Elevation gain and loss:** 140 feet.
**Trailhead elevation:** 2,500 feet.
**High point:** Umpqua, 2,640 feet.
**Maps:** Forest Service Trail 1414 printout, Umpqua National Forest.

**Finding the trailhead:** Follow the directions above to Thorn Prairie Road and follow it .6 mile to a grassy pullout on your left just before a bridge. This trail is so new that it isn't shown on the 1986 Toketee Falls and Potter Mountain USGS quads, but both the path and the springs are marked on the latest forest map.

**The hike:** The alternate route to Umpqua Hot Springs is included for those readers interested in sampling a slice of the recently built river trail which, when completed, will stretch from Idleyld Park on up to the Pacific Crest Trail near Maidu Lake—the headwaters of the North Umpqua River. It offers a pleasantly lonesome walk as well as a bit of exercise to make the hot soak even more welcome.

The well maintained trail climbs well above the canyon floor and undulates eastward through a forest of western red cedar and Douglas-fir. The roar of the river follows you, but the screen of trees hides it from view most of the way. The route detours at the halfway point to cross Deer Creek a hundred feet upstream on a log bridge.

In 1.5 miles, the new short cut described above cuts in from the right just beyond a bare slope easily mistaken for the one below the springs. The combined route then climbs steeply above the river and contours the hillside through woods for the last .25 mile. Watch your footing on the slick rock around the shelter, or you'll end up with a cold plunge in the river instead of a hot bath in the "tub"!

---

# HIKE 1b  *Clearwater River Trail*

**General description:** A 3.4-mile round-trip (or 1.7-mile one way) riverside walk through an age-old forest, near Umpqua Hot Springs.
**Elevation gain and loss:** 200 feet.
**Trailhead elevations:** West end, 2,440 feet; east end, 2,640 feet.
**High point:** 2,640 feet.
**Maps:** Forest Service Trail 1490 printout, Umpqua National Forest.

**Finding either trailhead:** At Toketee Junction on State Route 138, take Forest Road 34 to the bottom of the hill. Bear right at the "Y" onto graded Forest Road 4776, the west entrance to Toketee Ranger Station. Drive .25 mile to a pullout on the right and the west trailhead marker. The east trail sign is found two miles farther up the road just before it rejoins the highway.

**The hike:** Clearwater River Trail meanders through a twilight forest along the riverbank. Shaded by a dense canopy of cedar and Douglas-fir mixed with rhododendrons, alder, and dogwood, it passes lively rapids interspersed with deep pools. The gentle path parallels Toketee Ranger Station Road and can be walked from either end.

---

# HIKE 1c  *Toketee and Watson Falls*

**General description:** Two last short strolls through lush woods, near Umpqua Hot Springs.
**Elevation gain and loss:** Toketee Falls, 60 feet; Watson Falls, 230 feet.

**High points:** Toketee Falls, 2,380 feet; Watson Falls, 2,950 feet.
**Maps:** Forest Service Trail 1496 and 1495 printouts, Umpqua National Forest.

**Finding the trailheads:** To see Toketee Falls, drive to Toketee Junction on State Route 138 and take Forest Road 34 to the bottom of the hill. Bear left at the "Y" and follow signs to the parking area. To visit Watson Falls, drive 2.2 miles east of Toketee Junction on State Route 138 (or .3 mile east of the east entrance to Toketee Ranger Station) and follow signs to the picnic area parking lot.

**The hikes:** Toketee Falls, a double waterfall plunging a total of 120 feet, lies at the end of an easy .4-mile path along the North Umpqua River near Toketee Lake. At one spot, the river tumbles through a tight gorge filled with water sculpted pools. Mottled sunlight filters through a colorful grove of Douglas-fir, cedar, maple, and Pacific yew en route to a viewing platform.

Watson Falls, with its 272-foot drop, is the second highest waterfall in Oregon. A steep .6-mile trail follows the plunging creek through an age-old forest of Douglas-fir and western hemlock. The understory of ferns, Oregon grape, and salal blends tints of green with the velvet coat of moss draped over the creekside boulders. A footbridge along the way offers an excellent viewpoint, and the path comes to rest in the misty spray at the base of the falls.

# HIKE 1a *Umpqua Hot Springs via North Umpqua Trail*
# HIKE 1b *Clearwater River Trail*
# HIKE 1c *Toketee and Watson Falls*

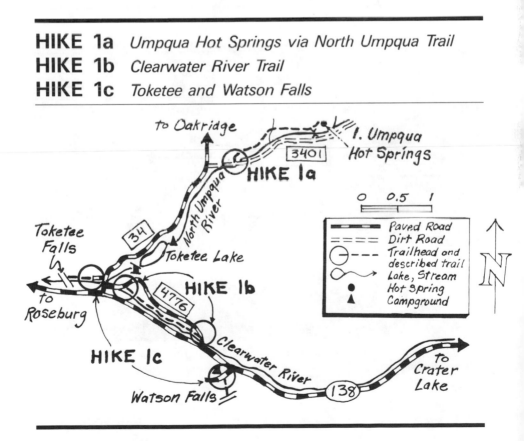

# 2 Wall Creek Warm Springs

**General description:** A warm soak in a sylvan setting at the end of a short path, southeast of Eugene in the Willamette National Forest. Swimwear optional. Elevation 2,200 feet.

**Directions:** From Eugene, drive about 40 miles southeast on State Route 58 to Oakridge. Turn left to city center, then right on East 1st which soon becomes Salmon Creek Road (Forest Road 24). Continue northeast, past Salmon Creek Campground, on pavement. At about nine miles, turn left on a gravel road (Forest Road 1934) signed "to Blair Lake". Watch for a pullout on your left in .4 mile, then follow an unmarked, .3-mile path up Wall Creek to the pool. The springs are marked without a name on the forest map.

**The warm springs:** A clearing in a virgin forest reveals a pool, also (aptly) called Meditation, built directly over the source springs. Bubbles rise gently to the surface in long streamers, warming the water to around 90 degrees. The newly built, rectangular pool (roughly 10 by 15 feet) sits on the bank of a small but lively creek. Surrounded by countless acres of green solitude, the setting more than makes up for the somewhat less-than-optimum bath temperature.

*Bubbles perk up through the sandy bottom of a pool bordered by age-old trees at Wall Creek Warm Springs*

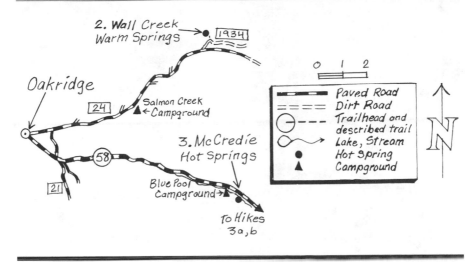

# 3 McCredie Hot Springs

**General description:** A highway pit stop that puts McDonalds and Burger King in the minor leagues, southeast of Eugene in Willamette National Forest. A strong skinnydipping tradition despite visibility. Elevation 2,100 feet.

**Directions:** Drive about 10 miles southeast of Oakridge on State Route 58 (.5 mile past Blue Pool Campground) to a parking loop on your right. An unsigned 40-yard path heads upstream to the pools. McCredie is named on the forest map.

**The hot springs:** This soaker-saturated site, sandwiched between a broad creek and a major highway, offers a variety of bubbly pools with temperatures ranging from 95-105 degrees. The "party pool" checks in at 15 by 20 feet and has a knee-deep bottom varying from sandy muck to sharp rocks and bits of glass.

Anytime is party time at McCredie; the action varies from mild, on weekdays, to industrial strength on weekends and after dark. Easily accessible year around, you're likely to find Winnebago City assembled in the large parking area. A nearby vantage point frequently houses a lineup of truck drivers-cum-birdwatchers.

A few slightly cooler (and quieter) pools may be found directly across the creek. To reach these with dry feet, drive another .5 mile up the highway and turn right on Shady Gap Road. Cross a bridge and bear right for .1 mile, then hunt for an overgrown path that follows the creek .25 mile back downstream.

*The "party pool" at McCredie Hot Springs sees few moments as tranquil as this.*

# HIKE 3a  *Fuji Mountain*

**General description:** A brisk 3-mile, round-trip day climb to a mountaintop overlooking a long line of volcanic peaks, near McCredie Hot Springs.
**Elevation gain and loss:** 964 feet.
**Trailhead elevation:** 6,180 feet.
**High point:** Fuji Mountain, 7,144 feet.
**Maps:** Diamond Peak Wilderness (Forest Service contour map) or Waldo Lake 7.5-minute USGS quad; Willamette National Forest.

**Finding the trailhead:** Drive about 15 miles southeast of Oakridge (or 5.5 miles past McCredie) on State Route 58. Watch for a train trestle over the highway and turn left just beyond it onto Eagle Creek Road (Forest Road 5883). With the help of the forest or wilderness map, follow this gravel road for 10.3 miles uphill to a small trail sign on the left and an equally small pullout on the right.

**The hike:** With a peak named Fuji, how can you miss? The short climb is a piece of cake, and the summit offers an overview of no less than three of the wilderness areas that now link the Oregon Cascades in an almost unbroken line. The route described here is a short cut to the summit overlooked by most hikers.

The lightly used path (3674) climbs moderately to a signed junction in .25 mile, then traverses along the west side of a steep ridge in a gentle climb through tall stands of mountain hemlock and true fir coated with tufts of moss. The last .5 mile is a steeper grade eased by switchbacks. Snow patches often obscure the route until mid-July.

Looking south from the summit, snow-capped Diamond Peak presides over the Diamond Peak Wilderness (see Hike 3b). Waldo Lake, framed by a landscape of wooded knolls and ridges, spreads out directly below. Fuji Mountain itself forms the southern boundary of the new 39,200-acre Waldo Lake Wilderness. The massive Three Sisters Wilderness lies just beyond it to the northeast; the glacier-capped peaks of the North and South Sisters, along with several other volcanic cones, can be spotted in a straight line fading into the distance.

# HIKE 3a *Fuji Mountain*

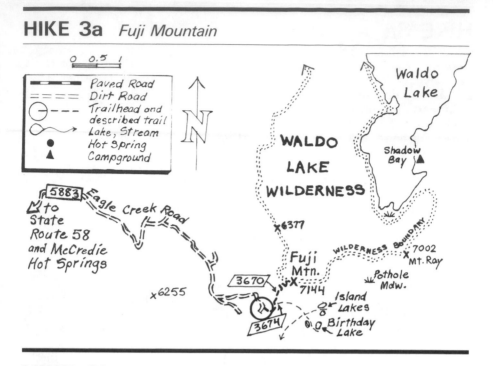

0 0.5 1

Paved Road
Dirt Road
Trailhead and described trail
Lake, Stream
Hot Spring
Campground

to State Route 58 and McCredie Hot Springs

5883

Eagle Creek Road

×6377

WALDO LAKE WILDERNESS

Waldo Lake

Shadow Bay

×6255

3670

Fuji Mtn.

×7144

3674

WILDERNESS BOUNDARY

×7002 Mt. Ray

Pothole Mdw.

Island Lakes

Birthday Lake

# HIKE 3b *Diamond Creek Loop and Vivian Lake*

**General description:** A moderate 6.5-mile, round-trip day hike (including a 2.25-mile loop) featuring waterfalls, wildflowers, and a wooded lake in the Diamond Peak Wilderness, near McCredie Hot Springs.

**Elevation gain and loss:** 1,486 feet (loop, 280 feet; 1,206 feet to Vivian Lake).

**Trailhead elevation:** 4,000 feet.

**High point:** Vivian Lake, 5,406 feet.

**Maps:** Diamond Peak Wilderness (Forest Service contour map) or Diamond Peak 7.5-minute USGS quad; Willamette National Forest.

**Finding the trailhead:** Drive about 22 miles southeast of Oakridge (or 12 miles past McCredie) on State Route 58, through the tunnel to Salt Creek Falls Viewpoint and trailhead parking.

**The hike:** A pleasant half-day outing through a shaded forest bursting with rhododendrons leads to waterfalls and a wooded lake. The first mile is part of a newly constructed 2.25-mile loop trail (not yet marked on the maps) to Diamond Creek Falls. The route described here combines the new loop with a 4.25-mile, round-trip extension from the far end south to Vivian Lake.

Vivian Lake Trail (3662) bridges Salt Creek and begins a gentle climb in a forest of hemlock and Douglas-fir. Thickets of bright pink rhododendrons and the solitary white blooms of bear grass highlight the way. The new route crosses a dirt road in .5 mile and once again just before reaching the far end of the loop.

Take the left fork at the junction to reach Vivian Lake. After crossing the

24

# HIKE 3b  *Diamond Creek Loop and Vivian Lake*

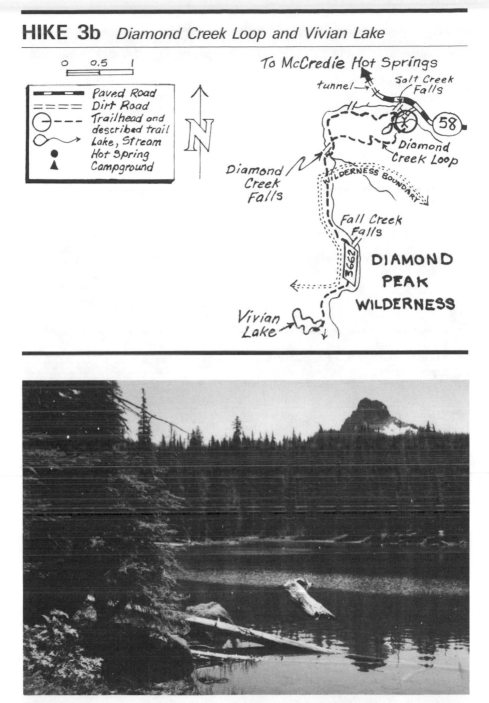

*The band of trees around Vivian Lake hides all but the tip of one of Mt. Yoran's angular lava crags.*

same road once more, followed by the Southern Pacific Railroad tracks and then yet another road, you'll welcome the final crossing—the wilderness boundary line! Next, the trail climbs a steep grade beside Fall Creek Falls, then tapers off a bit in the last .5 mile along the rushing creek. Thick woods hide the lake until the last minute.

The Diamond Peak Wilderness has expanded to presently cover 52,337 acres centered on the snow-crowned roots of an old volcano (8,744-foot Diamond Peak) and the 7,100-foot and 7,138-foot lava crags of Mt. Yoran. The peaks are flanked by forested ridges, tree-rimmed lakes, and a multitude of lakelets gouged out by glaciers.

Vivian Lake, a relatively small lake marked by an irregular shoreline, sits in a shallow basin walled in by trees. A few tiny clearings offer possible campsites or picnic areas. Looking across the green water, Mt. Yoran peeks an angular head above the treetops a couple of miles south.

Retrace your steps back to the junction and bear left on Diamond Creek

*A visitor at Cougar Hot Springs, if so inclined, can take a cold shower between hot soaks.*

Trail to complete the loop. The path soon reaches a broad, close range overlook of Upper Diamond Creek Falls. The second viewpoint is found via a spur that drops down to bridge the creek and return upstream to the base of the falls. The homeward route offers a few more vistas across the rugged canyon and a short spur to the rhododendron-rimmed shore of Too Much Bear Lake. Be sure to see Salt Creek Falls, another mighty plunge, before leaving the area.

---

# 4 Cougar Hot Springs

**General description:** An idyllic chain of (too) well known soaking pools reached by a short path near Cougar Reservoir, east of Eugene in Willamette National Forest. Highly skinnydippable. Elevation 2,000 feet.

**Directions:** From Eugene, drive about 42 miles east on State Route 126 to Blue River. Continue four miles to paved Forest Road 19 and follow it along the west side of Cougar Reservoir. At 7.5 miles, you'll pass a lagoon with a waterfall on your right followed by a parking area on the left. Walk back down the road and look for an unmarked trail just past the lagoon. The well worn, .3-mile path hugs the north shore, then climbs through a darkening forest to the pools. Cougar (once known as Terwilliger) isn't marked on the forest map.

**The hot springs:** Enveloped in the dark hues of a primeval woodland, Cougar is brushed by the mottled light filtering down from treetops high above. Five clear soaking pools spaced apart by giant logs are laid out in steps down a steep ravine. Spring water tumbles directly into the uppermost and hottest pool, and cold water flowing down a log flume provides an eye opening shower. Each rock and gravel pool is slightly cooler than the one above; they range in temperature from 108 down to 95 degrees. The moss coated trunk of one ancient log spanning the cleft plays host to a budding growth of ferns.

A volunteer group working with the Forest Service has built log steps and railings down the precipitous bank, and a resident caretaker is there to help protect and maintain the fragile area—a difficult job due to increasing use and abuse. If you value a pristine environment, please observe the basics: no soap or shampoo, no glass containers, pack out what you pack in, and be kind to the soil by staying on the established walkways. Cougar needs all the help it can get.

# HOT SPRINGS 4 *Cougar Hot Springs*

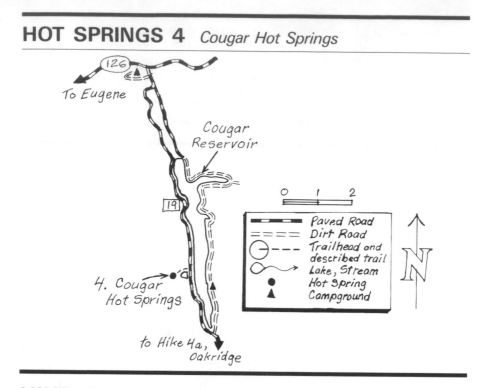

# HIKE 4a *Rebel Creek/Rebel Rock Loop*

**General description:** A fairly strenuous 12.5-mile, loop day hike climbing through a lonesome slice of the Three Sisters Wilderness, near Cougar Hot Springs.
**Elevation gain and loss:** 3,271 feet.
**Trailhead elevation:** 2,040 feet.
**High point:** 5,311 feet.
**Maps:** Three Sisters Wilderness (Forest Service contour map) or McKenzie Bridge and Chucksney Mtn. 15-minute USGS quads; Willamette National Forest.

**Finding the trailhead:** Follow the directions above to Cougar and continue south 6.5 miles (14 miles total from State Route 126). The parking loop is on the left, and the newly combined trailhead splits a short way above.

**The hike:** There has been more volcanic activity in the area of the Three Sisters Wilderness during the past few thousand years than in any other part of the entire Cascade range. The Three Sisters are the star attractions in this 285,202-acre wildland: The striking peaks with their 14 separate glaciers draw a multitude of climbers, hikers, and sightseers along boot-beaten paths to the east and north, while the western side remains relatively free of crowds.

The Rebel Creek/Rebel Rock Loop offers a quiet route stretching through virgin backcountry. Rebel Creek Trail climbs from creekside greenery and old-

*A primeval forest does battle with the faint path slicing through it on the Rebel Creek/Rebel Rock Loop.*

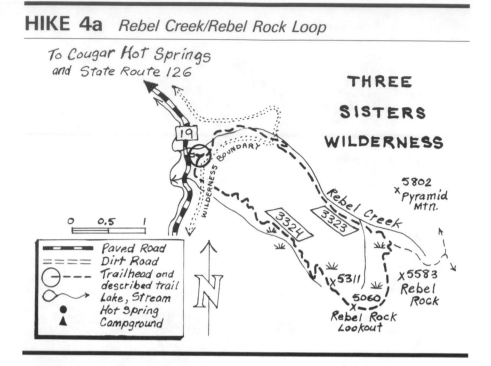

growth trees up through meadows dotted with pine and fir. It connects with Rebel Rock Trail, a ridgetop route offering rear balcony views of the Three Sisters and Mt. Jefferson before circling back down through more meadows and woods to end at the original trailhead.

It's best to follow Rebel Creek Trail up and Rebel Rock Trail back, as the elevation gain is more gradual this way. Turn left just above the parking loop onto Rebel Creek Trail (3323). Ferns and thimbleberries overgrow the path, and ancient stands of Douglas-fir, cedar, and western hemlock wrap it in many shades of green. It's a gentle climb southeast along the creek, and the only two crossings are on split-log bridges. The trail gradually leaves the creek and begins a moderate 5.7-mile climb to a junction in a grassy area at 4,480 feet.

Take the right fork, Rebel Rock Trail (3324), and climb one more ridge. You'll pass the base of 5,583-foot Rebel Rock while slicing through fields of knee-high flowers. The high meadows are peppered with mountain hemlock and true fir. As the ridgeline route slowly curves, it offers a variety of views en route to a large meadow on a 5,311-foot plateau. From here you can gaze out across the wilderness to several of the highest distant peaks.

It's all downhill from this point. The path plunges through more meadows so overgrown that the route is barely visible until you reach the lower woods. Here, hundreds of invisible spiderwebs span the trail between anchoring trees, ignoring the hiker's right of way. Ferns and thimbleberries again choke the path, and the forest closes in overhead.

# 5 Bigelow Hot Spring

**General description:** A secret soaking pool in a fern-laden grotto on the McKenzie River near a paved road, northeast of Eugene in the Willamette National Forest. Naked bodies welcome. Elevation 2,000 feet.

**Directions:** Take State Route 126 about 19 miles east and north of Blue River (four miles past Belknap Springs). Turn left onto paved Forest Road 2654 at .4 mile past milepost 15. Cross the river and park just past the bridge. Follow the signed McKenzie River Trail a short way south and watch for the second faint path heading down the steep bank to the river's edge. Bigelow isn't marked on the forest map.

**The hot spring:** This little jewel, well camouflaged among the many look-alikes along the riverbank, is a closely guarded secret. Rafting downstream, it would never catch your eye. Walking right above it on McKenzie River Trail (Hike 5a), you wouldn't see the pool through the trees. Even driving across the nearby bridge and looking right at it, there are no telltale signs to give it away unless it's occupied.

With the inlet at the bottom of the bubbly pool, hot water seeps in quietly to provide an optimum soaking temperature of 102 to 104 degrees. Riverside rocks line the outer edge, while the inner side forms a small grotto carved out

*Bigelow Hot Springs bubbles up from below into a fern grotto pool well hidden along the riverbank.*

of the steep riverbank. Luxuriant ferns overhang the pool, and moisture condenses overhead to drip back down on the steaming surface in cool droplets.

# HIKE 5a  *McKenzie River National Recreation Trail*

**General description:** A variable-length riverside stroll in the Willamette National Forest featuring virgin forests, lava flows and waterfalls, near Bigelow Hot Spring.
**Elevation gain and loss:** up to 1,750 feet.
**Trailhead elevation:** 1,450 feet.
**High point:** Clear Lake, 3,200 feet.
**Maps:** Forest Service brochure, Willamette National Forest.

**Finding the trailheads:** Drive about 52 miles east from Eugene on State Route 126 to McKenzie Ranger Station, where you can pick up a free brochure/map listing the many trailheads and exact mileages between points.

**The hike:** The riverside path above Bigelow Hot Spring is part of the 27-mile McKenzie River National Recreation Trail. The scenic route closely follows the whitewater river that originates in the high Cascades. Beginning just west of McKenzie Ranger Station and ending near Clear Lake and the river's headwaters, the route is a gentle climb upvalley parallel to State Route 126. There are 11 parking areas along the way that provide a variety of easy access points at signed trailheads.

*Graceful log bridges are a common sight along the McKenzie River Trail.*

The lower eight to 10 miles are usually free of snow year around. The hiker treads through dim forests of 600-year old Douglas-fir mixed with hemlock, cedar, and dogwood. Thick mats of Oregon grape, wildflowers, and salal crowd beneath vine maple and other hardwoods. The upper part passes areas where lava flows once spewed from nearby craters, filling the McKenzie Canyon and forcing the once mighty river through underground channels (see Hike 5b). Tamolitch, a broad valley of lava, remains a dry watercourse except in times of heavy runoff.

Above Tamolitch Valley, the trail passes two impressive waterfalls created by lava. Koosah Falls, a 70-foot drop into a deep pool, is outclassed by magnificent Sahalie Falls, a broad 100-foot plunge over a lava dam followed by a series of cascades that tumble another 40 feet. Clouds of spray billow outward over green banks.

Clear Lake, the next to last stop, was created some 3,000 years ago when a giant lava flow dammed the river and caused the wide valley upstream to fill in. You can see submerged trees through the clear surface near the north end-well preserved due to the icy, mineral-free water. Springs that average 43 degrees act as outlets for the buried river and well up from below to feed the lake. Great Springs, one of the largest, can be seen from the trail on the northeast side.

The McKenzie River Trail finally comes to rest near the Old Santiam Wagon Road just north of Clear Lake. This was the historic route over the Santiam Pass which became an early link between the mid-Willamette Valley and the lands in central and eastern Oregon.

# HIKE 5b  *The Blue Hole and Tamolitch Falls*

**General description:** A 4-mile, round-trip stroll to uncover one of the stranger sights along the McKenzie River Trail, near Bigelow Hot Spring.
**Elevation gain and loss:** 240 feet.
**Trailhead elevation:** 2,160 feet.
**High point:** The Blue Hole, 2,440 feet.
**Maps:** Same as Hike 5a.

**Finding the trailhead:** One could walk upstream to the Blue Hole from Bigelow, a pleasant round trip of 14 miles, but there's a much closer access point. Drive five miles farther north to Trail Bridge Reservoir. Cross the bridge to a junction and bear right. Where the road makes a sharp left, watch for a small turnout and trail marker.

**The hike:** One of the highlights on the McKenzie River Trail (Hike 5a) is a spot known locally as "the Blue Hole"—a brilliant blue pool of icy water that marks the place where the river rises from its underground channel, near the south end of Tamolitch Valley, to continue its course in a more normal fashion. It's quite a sight to see this strange pool, with no visible inlet, channeling out into a whitewater river.

Follow the McKenzie River Trail north for an easy two miles through deep woods. At one point, you'll cross a fern-laden marsh on a curving bridge hewn

# HOT SPRING 5  *Bigelow Hot Spring*
# HIKE 5a  *McKenzie River National Recreation Trail*
# HIKE 5b  *The Blue Hole and Tamolitch Falls*

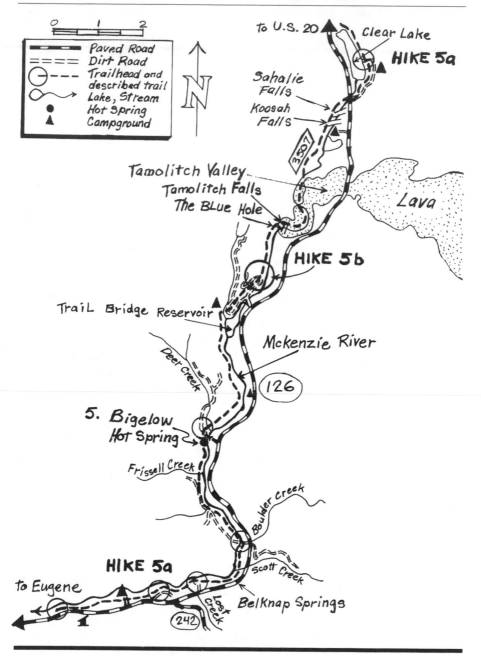

*The McKenzie River surfaces abruptly from its underground water course through "the Blue Hole."*

from logs. The route gradually emerges into the open at Tamolitch, the Valley of Lava. A drier landscape prevails across a riverbed of moss-coated volcanic rock that culminates in a 60-foot dropoff into the Blue Hole. Called Tamolitch Falls on the Forest Service brochure, the bone-dry cliff would confound any camera-clicking sightseer out to capture one more waterfall on film. But so would a river flowing downstream from nowhere!

# 6 Bagby Hot Springs

## HIKE 6a *To Bagby Hot Springs*

**General description:** A delightful 3-mile, round-trip day hike through lush woods to the Shangri-la of hot soaks, a treasure buried southeast of Portland in Mt. Hood National Forest. No need to pack a swimsuit.
**Elevation gain and loss:** 190 feet.
**Trailhead elevation:** 2,080 feet.
**High point:** Bagby, 2,270 feet.
**Maps:** Bagby Hot Springs 7.5-minute USGS quad; Mt. Hood National Forest.

**Finding the trailhead:** Bagby Hot Springs, located 70 miles southeast of Portland, is reached by following State Route 224 to Estacada and on into the Mt. Hood Forest. Take a right on Forest Road 46 at .5 mile past Ripplebrook Ranger Station, and bear right in 3.5 miles onto Forest Road 63. Turn right again in 3.5 miles onto Forest Road 70 and drive six miles to the trailhead parking lot. The roads are paved and well signed, and Bagby is marked on the forest map.

**The hike:** For the ultimate experience in natural hot springs, come to Bagby. A talented group of volunteers working with the Forest Service has built three rustic bathhouses, fed by two nearby springs, in a sylvan forest setting. The tubs are drained and cleaned daily by the hardworking Friends of Bagby who have also been adding decks with log benches, an outhouse, pathways, and landscaping. This unique group welcomes anyone interested in helping them preserve the area; they intend to keep Bagby open to the public and free through volunteer labor. You can send donations or apply for membership to Friends of Bagby, Inc., P.O. Box 15116, Portland, OR 97215.

The 1.5-mile Bagby Trail (544) is a delight in itself as it undulates through a grand old forest of Douglas-fir and cedar with an understory of vine maple. Moss-coated logs litter the way, and the path slices between cross sections with 5-foot diameters. The gentle creekside route passes emerald green pools spaced between rapids. Cross two bridges, then leave the creek behind just beyond the second to climb a short hillside to the springs.

The bathhouse at the upper spring, built in 1983, has a single 6-foot round cedar tub enclosed by minimum walls and maximum trees. The ceiling is pure sky. This is the spot for a family or cozy group to enjoy total privacy. A log flume 150 feet long diverts the 135-degree spring water into the tub, and a crude faucet admits cold water.

The communal bathhouse, finished in 1984, is another minimum wall/maximum tree and sky affair but on a larger scale. Three huge cedar logs, hollowed out to form long and narrow soaking tubs, are spaced a few feet apart; these

*In the communal bathhouse at Bagby Hot Springs are three hand-hewn soaking tubs hollowed out from giant logs.*

# HIKE 6a  *To Bagby Hot Springs*

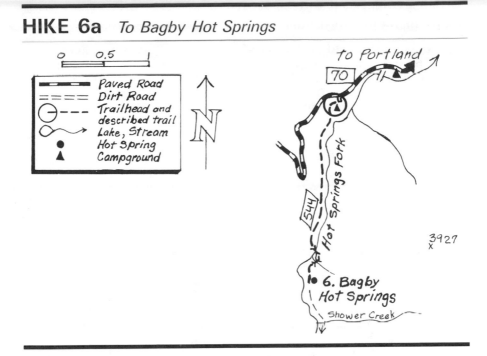

rustic log tubs are all that remain from the original bathhouse that burned down in 1979. At one end of the airy room is another 6-foot round tub. An adjoining bathhouse, completed in 1986, is a fully roofed replica of the one that burned; it offers five hand-hewn log tubs in private rooms.

A cleverly designed system of log flumes channels 135-degree water from the lower spring into each tub, and individual gates may be opened or closed to control the flow. Tub water drains out through another set of gates into long troughs that run beneath each house. One last flume feeds cold water into a centrally located well, and buckets are provided to carry it to the tubs.

Overnight camping isn't permitted at Bagby but is allowed at Shower Creek .5 mile farther on. At Spray Creek, 2.5 miles from the Bagby trailhead, the path enters the Bull of the Woods Wilderness. It continues through more verdant scenery, climbing 1,330 feet in the next eight miles to Silver King Mountain. From a high point at 4,600 feet along a ridge, you could drop east on Trail 573 to reach Twin Lakes in another two miles.

# HIKE 6b  *Bull of the Woods*

**General description:** An easy 6.5-mile, round-trip day hike to a lookout in the Bull of the Woods Wilderness with a view of Mt. Jefferson and Mt. Hood, not far from Bagby Hot Springs.
**Elevation gain and loss:** 963 feet.
**Trailhead elevation:** 4,560 feet.

**High point:** Bull of the Woods, 5,523 feet.
**Maps:** Bull of the Woods 7.5-minute USGS quad; Mt. Hood National Forest.

**Finding the trailhead:** Follow the directions above to the junction of Forest Roads 63 and 70 (the turnoff to Bagby) and continue two miles south on 63. Turn right on Forest Road 6340 and climb a gradually deteriorating surface to a 3-way junction in 10 miles. Take the rough spur farthest to the right and drive .4 mile to a small pullout and trail sign near the road end. Park here and put your boots to work.

**The hike:** What is Bull of the Woods? Take a short walk and see for yourself. The manned lookout that caps 5,523-foot Bull of the Woods is the logical spot to survey one of Oregon's newer wildlands. The 34,900-acre Bull of the Woods Wilderness, established in 1984, is a spoonful of wooded lakes spread out around the central peak. The small area, which includes the headwaters of the Collawash, Breitenbush, and North Santiam rivers, adds yet another link in the chain of wilderness gems running through the Cascades. The broad view from the summit includes many prominent peaks.

Follow Bull of the Woods Trail (550) on a gentle climb through a forest of Douglas-fir and western hemlock. Rhododendron, bear grass, and lupine brush the path in alternating bursts of pink, white, and blue/purple. The southward route hugs the west side of a ridge topped by North and South Dickey Peaks; it's basically one short and sweet traverse with a couple of hairpins at the end that offer previews of coming attractions.

The lookout has an expanse of open views of glacier-draped peaks from the Three Sisters north to Mt. Rainier. Most prominent is the angular white face of Mt. Jefferson standing out at 10,495 feet to the southeast. The massive shape of 11,239-foot Mt. Hood rises dramatically to the northeast. A pleasant loop may be made from the lookout east to the Welcome Lakes (Hike 6c).

*The lookout tower on top of Bull of the Woods offers an expanse of undulating mountain ranges dotted with volcanic cones.*

# HIKE 6b  *Bull of the Woods*
# HIKE 6c  *Bull of the Woods to the Welcome Lakes Loop*

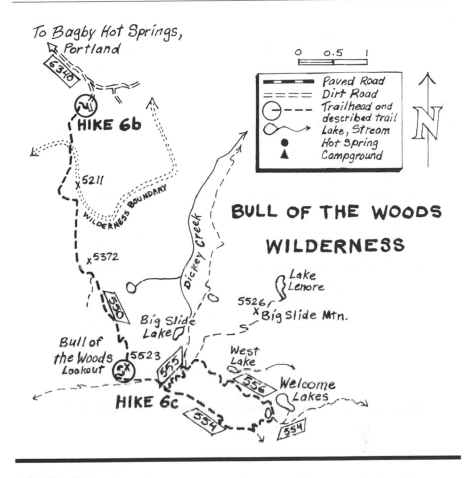

## HIKE 6c  *Bull of the Woods to the Welcome Lakes Loop*

**General description:** A moderate 5-mile, round-trip day hike or overnighter (including a 3.3-mile loop) from the lookout to lakes and more views of Bull of the Woods Wilderness, not far from Bagby Hot Springs.
**Elevation gain and loss:** 1,243 feet (283 feet to start of loop; loop, 960 feet).
**High point:** Trailhead, 5,523 feet.
**Low point:** Upper Welcome Lake, 4,440 feet.
**Maps:** Same as Hike 6b.

**Finding the trailhead:** Follow Hike 6b to Bull of the Woods.

**The hike:** The Welcome Lakes Loop makes a pleasant side trip from Bull of the Woods Lookout down through a bit more backcountry east of the summit. The 5-mile circuit passes through old-growth timber and open ridges, and it intersects a network of trails en route that could keep a backpacker busy for days.

The route begins by dropping steeply south from the lookout through deep woods, then veering east over a rockslide area. A junction is reached in .9 mile, 280 feet below the summit, with Schreiner Peak Trail (555) plunging downhill on the left. To follow the loop in a clockwise direction, turn north here and descend a series of tight switchbacks past Dickey Creek Trail branching left down to Big Slide Lake. Continue beyond a pond to a junction with the lower trail to the Welcome Lakes.

Turn right onto West Lake Way (556) and drop gradually through low forest, traversing 250 feet above West Lake, treading an open rocky area with good views around the scenic basin. The path contours gently downhill along the face of a slope and rounds a corner to arrive at Upper Welcome Lake. Orbit the small lake to intersect the Welcome Lakes Trail at 2.7 miles.

Upper Welcome Lake sits on a ledge a few hundred feet from the trail with a large dry campsite nearby. The surface is brushed in late summer with the yellow blooms of pond lilies. From the viewpoint east of the lake, you can look 240 feet down onto Lower Welcome Lake. An unsigned spur heads down from the Welcome Lakes Trail to the larger lake, adding a mile round trip to the hike.

Turn onto Welcome Lakes Trail (554) for the second half of the loop. The path zigzags up a ridge through meadows and more rockslide areas, passing a junction with the Geronimo Trail veering off on the left to Elk Lake. The route makes a 160-foot dip, then rises to follow the crest northwest with views down into West Lake Basin and across to Big Slide Mountain to the northeast.

Pass the junction with Schreiner Peak Trail, taking care to bear right at one last junction .2 mile to the west, and retrace your steps back up the mountain. The scenic loop completes the tour of hot springs and hikes in Oregon. Onward from here into Washington.

# FOR MORE INFORMATION

Contact the following Forest Service district offices for current conditions of hiking trails, stream crossings, and access roads. Forest and wilderness maps may be purchased at any district office or from offices of adjoining national forests.

**Hikes 1a-c:** Diamond Lake District, Umpqua National Forest, HC 60, Box 101, Idleyld Park, OR 97447; 503/498-2531. Toketee Ranger Station, on Forest Road 4776 near Toketee Lake, provides handy free trail printouts.

**Hikes 3a,b:** Oakridge District, Willamette National Forest, 46375 Highway 58, Westfir, OR 97492; 503/782-2291.

**Hike 4a:** Blue River District, Willamette National Forest, Blue River, OR 97413; 503/822-3317.

**Hikes 5a,b:** McKenzie District, Willamette National Forest, McKenzie Bridge, OR 97413; 503/822-3381.

**Hikes 6a-c:** Estacada District, Mt. Hood National Forest, 595 NW Industrial Way, Estacada, OR 97023; 503/630-6861.

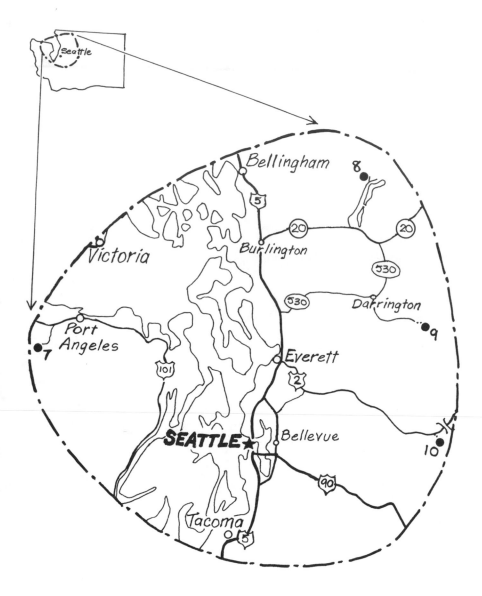

# WASHINGTON

## An Overview

Primitive hot springs on public land are surprisingly few and far between in the Evergreen State. The list might be much longer if it weren't for technical glitches like no useable soaking pools, no public access, buried by a river, or simply dried up and gone to hot spring heaven. However, the four shown on the Washington Locator Map have first-class soaking pools in totally magnificent hiking country. All are located either in national forests or parks; one gem resides in a craggy wilderness. Although they don't form a chain like those in Oregon or convenient clusters like the ones in Idaho, Washington's widely scattered bubblies are all well worth reaching.

The hot springs are found in two highly scenic and well travelled areas: the Olympic Mountains, which form the jagged core of the Olympic Peninsula, and the North Cascade range, with its many sharply sculpted glacial peaks. Both areas abound in craggy summits to rival the Swiss Alps, alpine meadows bursting with wildflowers, shrouded rain forests, and seething rivers with falls that thunder into vast canyons. The potential here is limited only by the hiker's imagination.

As a general rule, the forest access roads are paved and well signed, the campgrounds developed and heavily used, and the backcountry trails well maintained and teeming with other avid hot springers during the short summer months.

## Hot Springs and Hikes in Washington

We start the tour with a stroll to Olympic Hot Springs, the perfect base for alpine rambling in Olympic National Park (Hikes 7a-c). The remaining three springs are widely spaced within Mt. Baker-Snoqualmie National Forest on the verdant west side of the Cascade crest. Baker, the northernmost, has a year-around, easy-access pool and a classic climb in the nearby Mt. Baker National Recreational Area (Hike 8a). Next comes some in-depth coverage of the Glacier Peak Wilderness, with the hike-in hot box at Kennedy making an ideal base camp for high country treks (Hikes 9a-c). Last but not least is the short climb to Scenic, a hot dip near Stevens Pass, and a nearby hike in the Alpine Lakes Wilderness (Hikes 10a,b).

## Season

The high-country hiking season doesn't get comfortably underway until late in July, and even then blue skies can't be guaranteed. In an average year, the mountains west of the Cascade crest are cloud-free one day out of every six. The months of November through April bring torrents of rain to the lowlands and snow to higher elevations; intermittent storms are common through June and likely to return by early September. With the exception of Scenic and Olympic Hot Springs, which may be reached in the wintertime by experienced bushwhackers on snowshoes or X-C skis, all of the following hikes have a short midsummer season.

43

# 7 Olympic Hot Springs

## HIKE 7a  *To Olympic Hot Springs*

**General description:** An easy 5-mile, round-trip day hike or overnighter featuring popular soaking pools in a rain forest setting, southwest of Port Angeles in Olympic National Park. Skinnydippable after hours.
**Elevation gain and loss:** 260 feet.
**Trailhead elevation:** 1,800 feet.
**High point:** Olympic Hot Springs, 2,060 feet.
**Maps:** Seven Lakes Basin 15-minute USGS Custom Correct or Mt. Olympus Green Trails quads; Olympic National Park.

**Finding the trailhead:** Drive eight miles west of Port Angeles on U.S. Highway 101. Take Elwha River Road 10 miles south on pavement, past Elwha Ranger Station, to a roadblock and parking area at the signed trail. The springs are shown on the USGS quad.

**The hike:** Without a doubt the hot spot of the Olympics, this cluster of steaming springs, seeps, and pools lies sandwiched between a lush rain forest and the whitewater rapids of Boulder Creek. There are a total of seven bubbly

*The largest pool at Olympic Hot Springs mirrors a canopy of evergreens on a quiet summer day.*

soakers with a variety of sizes and temperatures to choose from—including one that overlooks a waterfall. A popular destination for day trippers, it's also the stepping off point for a variety of longer trips into the high Olympics (see Hikes 7b, c).

Situated high above the Elwha River Valley in Olympic National Park, the springs were at one time the site of a full-fledged resort. After the old buildings gave in to weather and neglect, washouts over the years closed part of the road. The Park Service has deliberately left the final stretch barred to motor vehicles in an attempt to curb too-heavy use of the fragile soaking pools.

According to an old Indian legend, two lightning fish (dragon-like creatures) fought a mighty battle here that neither could win, so they crawled into separate caves where they both still continue to shed hot bitter tears. The tears provide hot water at both Olympic and nearby Sol Duc Hot Springs (a modernized historic resort). The tears at Olympic range the gamut from lukewarm to 188 degrees.

Walk the last 2.2 miles of crumbling pavement, a gentle grade through deep woods, and set your pack down at Boulder Creek Campground. The short path from here to the springs drops down the hill, bridges Boulder Creek, then meanders on downstream passing one soaking pool after another.

A variety of side paths wriggle down the grassy bank and up into the forest; some hit the jackpot while others just circle around in a maze, reinforced by the steady tread of hopeful feet. Perseverance mixed with a dash of logic and luck will lead you to the more secluded pools.

The nearby campground is complete with flush toilets and piped water, picnic tables and fire grills, spacious tent sites, and even a communal pole to hang foodbags or backpacks out of reach from hungry bears. What nicer base camp could you find for the following hikes?

# HIKE 7b   *Olympic Hot Springs to Appleton Pass*

**General description:** A strenuous 10.5-mile, round-trip day hike or overnighter from the hot springs to alpine meadows and breathtaking views, in the northern mountains of Olympic National Park.
**Elevation gain and loss:** +2,920 feet, -120 feet.
**Trailhead elevation:** 2,200 feet at Boulder Creek Campground.
**High point:** Appleton Pass, 5,000 feet.
**Maps:** Same as Hike 7a.

**Finding the trailhead:** Follow Hike 7a to Olympic Hot Springs.

**The hike:** Olympic Hot Springs makes a great base for a side trip to Appleton Pass. This deservedly popular route climbs up, up, up through green meadows laced with wildflowers to an awesome view across High Divide. Wave after wave of snow-capped peaks recedes southward to the horizon like whitecaps on a stormy sea. Mount Olympus, at 7,965 feet, rides the highest crest. Airy campsites dot the pass, and a tempting extension of the route could be made from here across to Seven Lakes Basin and High Divide.

Appleton Pass Trail begins at the upper end of Boulder Creek Campground and winds through twilight woods to a junction in .7 mile with Boulder Lake Trail (Hike 7c). The gentle grade continues until the path bridges the North Fork of Boulder Creek. Now the work begins as the route shoots up the canyon of the South Fork of Boulder Creek. Two short spurs a short distance apart lead to cascading falls and a small campsite apiece while the main trail bridges the creek and climbs on.

Crunch your way along a path littered with the small cones of western hemlock and Douglas-fir mixed with a dash of cedar. Log walkways aid the traverse over fragile marshy areas to a large campsite at 2.5 miles. The route crosses several rockslides spaced between stands of subalpine fir and a wavy tangle of slide alder to finally emerge into a steep meadow.

A thick mat of summer wildflowers competes with huckleberry, willow, and other bushy plants in the waist-deep grass; the humid fragrance is intoxicating. Watch for fat marmots sunbathing on rocky outcrops as you work your way up. Beyond, you'll cross the South Fork twice and then climb to a high basin just below the pass.

Catch your breath and prepare for the last nine switchbacks up a precipitous slope that's often deep in snow until midsummer. An ice axe is well advised for early season hikers; a far easier snow climb from here crosses past tiny Oyster Lake up a long valley to a viewpoint .5 mile east of Appleton Pass.

Views from the pass itself are limited to tantalizing glimpses through the trees, so it's well worth the extra .5 mile and 300-foot gain to follow the ridgeline path east to the unnamed viewpoint. Tiny dwarfs of subalpine fir dot the plush green carpet spread out here, and the view unfolds in all directions. Mt. Carrie towers in the foreground to the southeast, and Mt. Appleton looms to the north.

*"Snow Joke":* *Fingers and toes half frozen from kicking one precarious step after another into crusty snow on the final steep pitch to Appleton Pass, my*

*Avalanche lilies carpet the viewpoint just east of Appleton Pass, and the jagged peaks along High Divide are seen to the south.*

*knees shook every time I made the mistake of glancing back down the slick wall. Concentrating instead on looking up, I began to see a sight that made me doubt my senses. A volley of snow-white balls was arcing through the blue sky above me, coming from some source just out of sight.*

*And there, as I hauled my stiff body onto the crest, wearing only faded cutoffs and sturdy boots, stood a talented snowball juggler practicing his art! He paused long enough to share a precious quart of milk, then gathered up a handful of white avalanche lilies which he promptly consumed for dessert. Then, with a cheerful wave, he leaped over the edge. I blinked twice and peered down just in time to see him disappear far below in a graceful glissade, using only his boots for skis.*

---

# HIKE 7c  *Olympic Hot Springs to Boulder Lake*

**General description:** A moderate 7-mile, round-trip day hike or overnighter from the hot springs to a tree-rimmed lake and high views, in the northern mountains of Olympic National Park.
**Elevation gain and loss:** 2,150 feet.
**Trailhead elevation:** 2,200 feet at Boulder Creek Campground.
**High point:** Boulder Lake, 4,350 feet.
**Maps:** Same as Hike 7a.

**Finding the trailhead:** Follow Hike 7a to Olympic Hot Springs.

**The hike:** Another pleasant outing from the hot springs, not as spectacular as that to Appleton Pass (Hike 7b) but less demanding, climbs to a small lake nestled in a wooded basin. The snowfields and cliffs of Boulder Peak rise 1,250 feet above the southwest shore, offering an additional challenge rewarded by excellent views.

Start toward Appleton Pass from Boulder Creek Campground and branch to the right in .7 mile onto Boulder Lake Trail. The route is a traverse climbing steadily above the North Fork of Boulder Creek, with a forest of Douglas-fir giving way to one of graceful western hemlock. Beyond Halfway Creek, the trail passes rockslide areas followed by stands of cedar and fir, crosses two rushing creeks, and finally levels off into a meadow at the head of the valley. Subalpine firs line the last short rise to the lake.

Boulder Lake has a level campsite (popular with fishermen) near the small peninsula on the north shore. The short climb from the lake to the 5,600-foot summit of Boulder Peak is steep but not difficult. The panoramic view at the top includes Mt. Appleton (nearby to the southeast) almost eclipsing massive Mt. Olympus in the distance, and 7,000-foot Mt. Carrie crowning the eastern end of High Divide.

# HIKE 7a  *To Olympic Hot Springs*
# HIKE 7b  *Olympic Hot Springs to Appleton Pass*
# HIKE 7c  *Olympic Hot Springs to Boulder Lake*

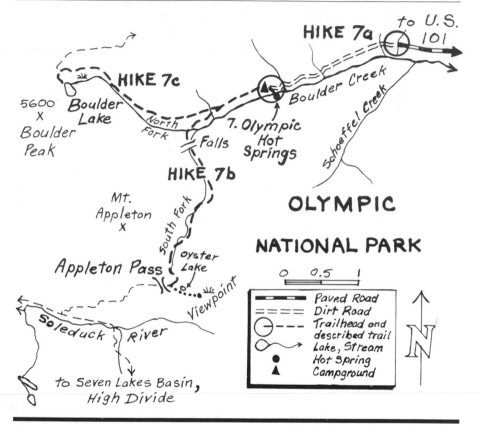

# 8 Baker Hot Springs

**General description:** A bather-full bubbly framed by evergreens at the end of a short path, northeast of Burlington in Mt. Baker-Snoqualmie National Forest. A bathing suit/birthday suit mix. Elevation 2,000 feet.

**Directions:** From Interstate 5 at Burlington, take State Route 20 about 23 miles east. Bear left onto paved Baker Lake Road and follow it up the west side of the lake. Make a sharp left opposite Baker Lake Resort onto a gravel road (Forest Road 1144) and climb 3.2 miles to a parking area. A sneaker-smoothed boardwalk paves most of the .3-mile path through a cool forest of western hemlock and cedar and emerges into a sunny clearing at the pool. Baker isn't marked on the forest map.

**The hot springs:** One large pool dug out of a sandy bank greets a long line

# HOT SPRINGS 8 *Baker Hot Springs*

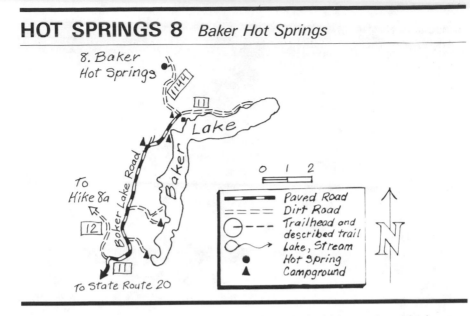

of happy soakers at Baker. Natural mineral water bubbles up from the bottom at about 109 degrees and cools as it disperses. Users have installed a moveable hose to divert cold water from a nearby stream.

At one time there was a wooden tub built over the springs, but the Forest Service was eventually forced to rip it out due to a high bacteria count brewing in the cedar walls. Only a small flow cleans the present pool; the water tends to be a bit on the cloudy side, but that doesn't seem to faze the aficionados who come for a hot soak. Unless you feel like sharing your cozy cocoon, try the early mornings or the off-season months.

# HIKE 8a *Park Butte*

**General description:** A strenuous 7-mile, round-trip day hike or overnighter featuring alpine meadows and close views of Mt. Baker, both from the lookout and from nearby railroad grade, not far from Baker Hot Springs.
**Elevation gain and loss:** +2180 feet, -80 feet.
**Trailhead elevation:** 3,350 feet.
**High point:** Park Butte Lookout, 5,450 feet.
**Maps:** Hamilton 15-minute USGS or Green Trails quads; Mt. Baker-Snoqualmie National Forest.

**Finding the trailhead:** Follow the directions above and drive just over 12 miles up Baker Lake Road. Turn left onto a gravel road signed "to Schreibers Meadow" (Forest Road 12) and in 3.5 miles bear right onto Forest Road 13. Climb 5.5 progressively bumpier miles to the road-end trail sign and park wherever you can. (For future reference, the trailhead is a 20-mile drive from Baker Hot Springs.)

*This party-size pool at Baker Hot Springs plays host every year to many congenial groups of soakers.*

*The railroad grade, a knife-edged moraine created by Mt. Baker's Easton Glacier, attracts seasoned scramblers along its knobby spine.*

**The hike:** This short climb in the Mt. Baker National Recreation Area is a hard one to beat for wall-to-wall alpine views. Snow-draped peaks rim the horizon, and the awesome sight of Mt. Baker's Easton Glacier steals the foreground. Lush meadows and tiny lakes are cupped between rocky knolls, and tumbling streams carve clefts between ridges and glacial moraines. Fat marmots announce your arrival with piercing cries.

Park Butte Trail (603) begins by bridging Sulphur Creek and undulating through Schriebers Meadow, where heather and huckleberries choke the open spaces and Mt. Baker glistens between scattered stands of cedar and fir. Beyond lies a moonscape of rock and rushing streams. Volcanic mudflows and meltwater from the massive Easton Glacier have sliced freeways through the forest here; you'll probably have to boulder-hop a bit to cross the channels, especially on warm summer afternoons.

# HIKE 8a  *Park Butte*

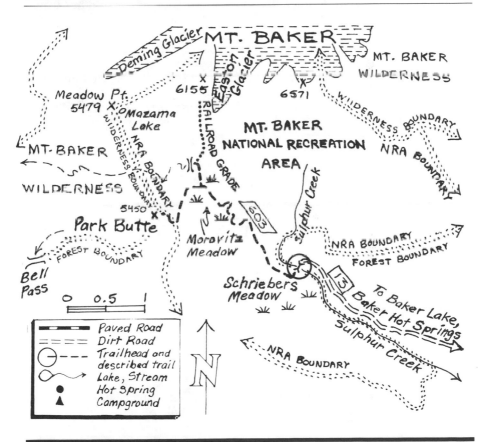

Next comes the hard part. The path, now wrapped in cool woods, gains 800 feet in a long and very steep mile to Lower Morovitz Meadow. Western hemlock gives way to mountain hemlock en route. Western red cedar yields to a strange looking cousin, the Alaska cedar, whose needles hang in long chains from drooping limbs. The off-white, shaggy bark peels off in long strips as if some bear had been using the poor tree as a sharpening post for giant claws!

The grade tapers on the way to Upper Morovitz Meadow where you'll find superb campsites amid alpine scenery. The main trail goes across the meadow past a junction, with increasing panoramas as it climbs the last mile south above Pocket Lake then west to the summit. The lookout cabin, leased by Skagit Alpine Club of Mt. Vernon, is available to the public when not being used by its members.

Park Butte, ringed by peaks far and near, will take your breath away just when you stop to catch it. The 10,778-foot white cone of Mt. Baker dominates the view. Its satellite peaks, the Black Buttes, jut above the Deming Glacier in sharp contrast. Looking westward, you'll see the serrated crests of the Twin Sisters range. To the south are Loomis Mountain and Dock Butte, backed in the far distance by Mt. Rainier. To the east and southeast rise other distant cones including snow-clad Glacier Peak (see Hikes 9a-c).

Returning to the junction in the upper meadow, there's another direction to go that's well worth exploring. Take the side trail north over Baker Pass and ramble northeast to intersect the long rocky spine of the railroad grade. Pick your way along the tip of this knife-edged ridge, a moraine built up by the nearby Easton Glacier.

You can gaze eastward across the giant cleft to the massive glacier and barren landscape below the ice or look up, as you're drawn ever closer, to the gleaming-white volcanic cone of Mt. Baker. Remote campsites hidden in clusters of subalpine fir speckle the high meadows west of the railroad grade, and further cross-country routes beckon.

---

# 9 Kennedy Hot Spring

## HIKE 9a  To Kennedy Hot Spring

**General description:** An easy 11-mile, round-trip day hike or overnighter featuring a bubbly soaking box in the Glacier Peak Wilderness, northeast of Everett. No need to pack a swimsuit.
**Elevation gain and loss:** +1,100 feet, -100 feet.
**Trailhead elevation:** 2,300 feet.
**High point:** Kennedy, 3,300 feet.
**Maps:** Glacier Peak 15-minute USGS or Green Trails quads, or Glacier Peak Wilderness (Forest Service contour map); Mt. Baker-Snoqualmie National Forest.

**Finding the trailhead:** To reach this alpine hideaway from Interstate 5, take State Route 530 about 32 miles east to Darrington. Turn right onto the Mountain Loop Highway (Forest Road 20) and drive 10 miles south along the Sauk

River. Turn left onto White Chuck Road (Forest Road 23) and drive 11 dusty miles to the road-end parking area and trail sign. Kennedy is named on all the maps.

**The hike:** Remember Badfinger singing "You'd better hurry 'cause it's going fast"? Well, Kennedy Hot Spring, currently down to 94 degrees, has been dropping about a degree every year according to one oldtimer who can remember when it was once 102. Despite the lukewarm temperature and a yellowish cast (iron oxide) to the water, Kennedy remains a favored goal for day trippers as well as a popular stopoff for longer distance trekkers on the nearby Pacific Crest Trail (PCT).

The Glacier Peak Wilderness surrounding Kennedy fills 576,865 prime acres of the North Cascades and forms the largest wildland in the state of

*The "standing room only" cedar box at Kennedy Hot Spring can accommodate a crowd of vertical soakers—including many who find their toes dangling in space.*

Washington. Measuring 35 miles long by 20 miles wide, it offers 450 miles of hiking trails. Most of the passes aren't snow-free before mid-August, but this varies from year to year. The PCT snakes through the heart of the wildland as it swings around Glacier Peak, Washington's fourth highest and most remote volcanic cone.

The White Chuck Trail (643), probably the most popular walk in the Glacier Peak area, winds gently up the canyon of the White Chuck River. An understory of ferns and vine maple flourishes under a ceiling of ancient cedar and Douglas-fir. The river can be constantly heard but only glimpsed through the trees. Side streams cross the path in a headlong rush to join the cascade below. At one point, the route drops to river level and passes a few campsites along a gravel beach; at another, it passes beneath pumice rockslides and cliffs of volcanic tuff.

Kennedy Ridge Trail branches left at five miles to climb up beside alpine meadows and glaciers (Hike 9b). The main trail soon bridges Kennedy Creek, intersects the spur branching right to the hot spring, then ends in 1.5 miles at a junction with the PCT. One could ramble south from this point through Glacier Peak Meadows and on over White Pass in another ten miles, or travel north to Kennedy Ridge past glaciers and tumbling streams to cross Fire Creek Pass and drop down to Milk Creek and the Suiattle River.

The short spur to the hot spring passes many campsites along and above the river; a cold spring at the guard station provides good drinking water. The path bridges the river to a junction: the right fork leads to more campsites, then shoots up to Lake Byrne (Hike 9c) and beyond; the left fork follows the river a short way upstream to reach Kennedy Hot Spring in a total of 5.5 miles.

The extraordinary soaker here consists of a 4-by-5-foot, cedar box recessed into the ground. As the depth is over five feet, the strategy is to do your soaking in a vertical position. A surprising number of bodies can squeeze into the small box in this unusual fashion—either standing up, if they're tall enough, or by just gripping the sides with toes suspended!

Spring water filters in through the rocky bottom and rises in warm bubbles to the surface. A small platform borders the box, with a handy rack nearby for clothes and towels. Nestled into the bank between the milky river and a wall of trees, Kennedy's magic bubble box offers highly scenic therapy for aching muscles.

It should be mentioned in passing that two other hot springs marked so temptingly on the wilderness map are reported to be wild goose chases. Gamma Hot Spring lies buried in a deep chasm miles from the nearest hiking trail. Sulphur Hot Spring, lost in another wild ravine, is now only a tepid, algae-coated mud puddle. Sorry, folks.

---

# HIKE 9b  *Kennedy Hot Spring to Glacier Creek Meadow*

**General description:** A moderate 9-mile, round-trip day hike or overnighter from the hot spring to high meadows and glacial icefalls, in the Glacier Peak Wilderness.

**Elevation gain and loss:** +2,450 feet, -100 feet.

**Trailhead elevation:** 3,300 feet at Kennedy.

*The rocky moraine above Glacier Creek Meadow offers hikers a close-up look at Scimitar and Kennedy glaciers just beneath 10,541-foot Glacier Peak*

**High point:** Glacier Creek Meadow, 5,650 feet.
**Maps:** Same as Hike 9a.

**Finding the trailhead:** Follow Hike 9a to Kennedy Hot Spring.

**The hike:** An exhilarating side trip from the hot spring climbs to an alpine meadow bisected by a gurgling glacier-fed stream. The grassy banks along the creek make an idyllic spot to sit and dangle hot toes in icy water, enjoy a picnic lunch, and contemplate the world around you. Head farther upvalley, if you can tear yourself away, for a face-to-face confrontation with nearby glaciers.

From Kennedy, retrace your steps .5 mile to the point where White Chuck Trail meets Kennedy Ridge Trail (639). Tree roots across the path form randomly spaced steps as the route climbs 875 feet in two miles to join the PCT at 4,150 feet. Continue on up the ridge with increasing glimpses through the trees of silvered glaciers and peaks. The PCT emerges into the lush meadow bordering Glacier Creek (at 5,650 feet) in another two miles.

The heather meadow bursts with lupine and glacier lilies. Marmots stare down from rocky castles, and tiny birds sing out from invisible perches. Glacier Creek ripples down the slope in rocky steps to form small pools between cascades. A campsite bedded in a plush-green carpet lies just downstream from the path.

The dark moraine above Kennedy Glacier juts into view at the head of the long meadow.

For a view of distant peaks and a close-up of two glaciers, leave the trail behind and follow the creek up beyond the valley. A faint climber's route leads up the side of a moraine and follows the rocky crest ever closer to the glistening 10,541-foot cone of Glacier Peak. Scimitar Glacier can be seen to the southeast, and the double tongue of Kennedy Glacier looms before you. Ribbons of water emerge from the base of the icefall to twist and braid their way downhill over glacial debris.

---

# HIKE 9c  *Kennedy Hot Spring to Lake Byrne*

**General description:** A grueling 5-mile, round-trip day hike or overnighter climbing from the hot spring to an alpine lake and panoramic vistas in the Glacier Peak Wilderness.
**Elevation gain and loss:** 2,250 feet.
**Trailhead elevation:** 3,300 feet at Kennedy.
**High point:** Lake Byrne, 5,550 feet.
**Maps:** Same as Hike 9a.

**Finding the trailhead:** Follow Hike 9a to Kennedy Hot Spring.

**The hike:** The bubble box at Kennedy makes the ultimate base for yet another outing, more demanding but every bit as rewarding as the climb to Glacier Creek Meadow (Hike 9b). Lake Byrne, nestled in a rock basin directly across the deep canyon of the White Chuck from Glacier Peak, offers a face-on view of the massive pyramid—that is, if the curtain of clouds parts far enough to let you look across! The short climb is a real backbreaker, but the spectacular scene is worth the price.

*Looking east from Lake Byrne, the massive cone of Glacier Peak can be seen across the canyon of the White Chuck River.*

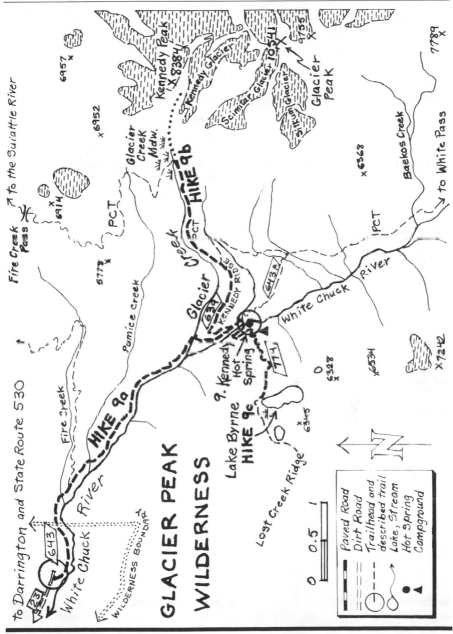

The Lake Byrne Trail (774) begins at the bridge by Kennedy. A relentless series of tight switchbacks drags the path straight up the canyon wall; luckily, the route is shaded by an obliging forest. In about 1.5 miles, the path levels off long enough to pivot southwest and then north around a sharp knoll, passing a heather dappled meadow with the first open views across the canyon. The final stretch of hairpins is open to both the sun's rays and increasingly broad panoramas. The path fords the gushing outlet to reach the northern tip of Lake Byrne in 2.5 miles.

Fragile meadows fringe one side of the oblong lake while scattered clusters of subalpine fir cling to outcrops of rock on the far side. Ice can often coat the deep blue lake (and snow obscure the trail) until mid-August. Camping is banned within .25 mile of Lake Byrne, but there are two good campsites north of the outlet and an unconventional, open-air privy near the trail.

Experienced scramblers can roam the steep ridges that wall the lake. The high knob at the south end offers one of the finest views in the North Cascades. Looking due east, 10,541-foot Glacier Peak fills the foreground. On a clear day, you can see the distant white cones of Mt. Baker (see Hike 8a) and Mt. Shuksan to the northwest. A combination of boot tread, tree blazes, and cross-country travel lures the more adventurous traveler westward from Lake Byrne to a chain of lakes and open meadows along Lost Creek Ridge.

# 10 Scenic Hot Springs

## HIKE 10a  *To Scenic Hot Springs*

**General description:** A rugged 4-mile, round-trip day hike featuring an aptly named gem hidden southeast of Everett near the Cascade crest. Naked bodies welcome.
**Elevation gain and loss:** 1,140 feet.
**Trailhead elevation:** 2,360 feet.
**High point:** Hot springs, 3,500 feet.
**Maps:** Scenic 7.5-minute USGS or Stevens Pass 15-minute Green Trails quads; Mt. Baker-Snoqualmie National Forest.

**Finding the trailhead:** From Everett, take U.S. Highway 2 about 50 miles southeast to Skykomish. Continue 10 miles to Scenic, the service depot for the Burlington-Northern Railroad's Cascade tunnel (see Hike 10b). Cross the highway bridge that spans the tracks and watch for a primitive road on your right .2 mile east of milepost 59. Unless you've got a high clearance vehicle, it's best to park wherever you can find a niche near the bottom and walk up. The springs aren't marked on any map.

**The hike:** Tucked away high on a hillside overlooking Windy Mountain and the broad canyon just west of Stevens Pass, Scenic Hot Springs lives up to its name. A user-built soaking box collects the flow, and evergreen branches frame the view. Used mainly by locals and a few wintertime ski buffs, it's bordered by Mt. Baker-Snoqualmie Forest and the northern tip of the Alpine

*At Scenic Hot Springs, hot water is fed through a hose into a user-built soaking box perched on the steep hillside.*

Lakes Wilderness. The springs and access route are on a tiny plot of private land within the forest, but the owners are reported to be a group of doctors who don't object to visitors as long as they continue to show respect for the property.

The rocky road climbs a steep .5-mile slope to a string of powerlines, then gets steeper and rockier yet as it turns to follow them eastward. Start counting from the first set of poles you come to, making sure you don't count the same pair twice as the track zigzags uphill. When you're about midway between the 4th and 5th, look for a faint path to the right which contours uphill in a .5-mile arc to the springs.

The waist deep, 4-by-6-foot soaking box commands an outstanding view. The 108-degree spring water can be cooled by diverting an incoming hose, and a copious flow keeps the water clean. This isn't the place for flipflops or treadless sneakers, as the ground around the springs is steep and slippery. Scenic Hot Springs, also known as Great Northern, feeds three smaller pools nearby in addition to the main tub.

# HIKE 10b  *Surprise Lake*

**General description:** A moderate 8-mile, round-trip day hike or overnighter climbing past waterfalls to the first in a group of secluded lakes in the Alpine Lakes Wilderness, near Scenic Hot Springs.
**Elevation gain and loss:** 2,300 feet.

## HIKE 10a *To Scenic Hot Springs*
## HIKE 10b *Surprise Lake*

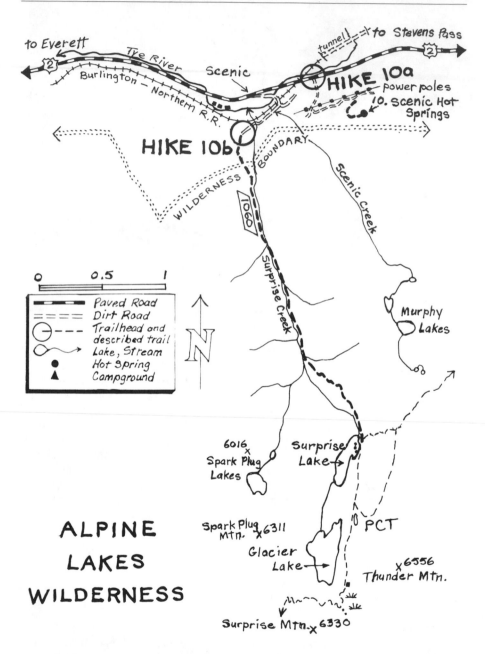

to Everett

Tye River

Scenic

tunnel

to Stevens Pass

Burlington — Northern R.R.

HIKE 10a

power poles

10. scenic Hot Springs

HIKE 10b

WILDERNESS BOUNDARY

Scenic Creek

1060

Surprise Creek

Murphy Lakes

0    0.5    1

Paved Road
Dirt Road
Trailhead and described trail
Lake, Stream
Hot Spring
Campground

N

6016
x
Spark Plug Lakes

Surprise Lake →

ALPINE

LAKES

WILDERNESS

Spark Plug
Mtn. x 6311

PCT

Glacier Lake →

x 6556
Thunder Mtn.

Surprise Mtn. x 6330

60

**Trailhead elevation:** 2,200 feet.
**High point:** Surprise Lake, 4,500 feet.
**Maps:** Same as Hike 10a.

**Finding the trailhead:** Follow the road access to Scenic given in Hike 10a. Turn right, .7 mile east of milepost 58, on an unmarked road that bridges the Tye River and drops down to cross the train tracks and intersect a side road. Turn right and drive about .25 mile to the parking area and trail sign.

**The hike:** An image of evergreenery walled in by white granite is mirrored in the glassy surface of Surprise Lake. Three tiny islands near the outlet stipple the reflection. The oblong lake lies at the end of a brisk 4-mile climb which soon joins the Pacific Crest Trail (PCT) and leads on to other alpine delights. What's the surprise? No telling—you'll just have to decide for yourself.

Surprise Creek Trail (1060) starts by swinging away from the creek in a moderate climb up an open hillside but swings back in .5 mile to enter cool woods along Surprise Creek. Soon shrouded under a canopy of age-old trees, it hugs the creek banks in a gentle 2.5-mile stretch upvalley past waterfalls and blue pools. Rocky walls slowly converge as the canyon narrows.

The final mile is a steep climb up the headwall in a series of tight hairpins that parallels the cataract of the rushing stream below. The old route of the PCT branches off to twist straight up the east canyon wall just before the path reaches the north tip of the lake at four miles.

Surprise Lake, nestled in a hanging valley flanked by cliffs, makes a delightful spot to enjoy a picnic lunch. For a longer trip, follow the trail .7 mile south to the PCT and on up to Glacier Lake, lying in a bowl of granite at the base of Surprise Mountain a mile beyond (and 300 feet above) Surprise Lake. Grassy campsites tempt the visitor to stay and explore the alpine basin or to climb the 6,330-foot peak for an overview of other lakes and mountains in the magnificent 305,407-acre Alpine Lakes Wilderness, Washington's third largest wildland.

# FOR MORE INFORMATION

Contact the following Forest Service district offices for current conditions of hiking trails, stream crossings, and access roads. Forest and wilderness maps may be purchased at any district office or from offices of adjoining national forests.

**Hikes 7a-c:** Elwha Ranger Station, Olympic National Park, 480 Olympic Hot Springs Road, Port Angeles, WA 98362; 206/452-9191.

**Hike 8a:** Mt. Baker District, Mt. Baker-Snoqualmie National Forest, Sedro Woolley, WA 98284; 206/856-5700.

**Hikes 9a-c:** Darrington District, Mt. Baker-Snoqualmie National Forest, Darrington, WA 98241; 206/436-1155.

**Hike 10b:** Skykomish District, Mt. Baker-Snoqualmie National Forest, Skykomish, WA 98288; 206/677-2414.

# HOT SPRINGS IN IDAHO

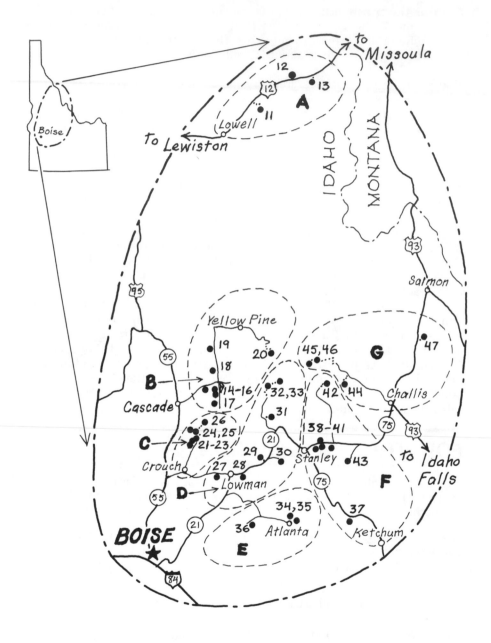

# IDAHO

## An Overview

It so happens that the state of Idaho contains more geothermal gems than all of the western states, British Columbia, and Alberta put together. The 37 shown on the Idaho Locator Map are all located in prime hiking areas in national forests. Half lie either near the edge or well within the boundaries of protected wilderness areas. And yet, surprisingly few backcountry buffs visit the Potato State. Even the spectacular Sawtooths, congested by Idaho's standards, seem delightfully deserted to hikers accustomed to fighting the summer crowds in the Cascades or the Olympics.

Compared to Oregon and Washington, the backcountry of Idaho is far less developed. Few forest roads are paved, many involve the time-consuming process of skirting rocks and potholes, and most cover vast distances in an endless cloud of dust. Campgrounds are mostly the undeveloped type and still free. The hikes often involve wading, log balancing, or rock hopping across unbridged streams. But Idaho's hot springs make up for any minor inconvenience. Most get relatively little use or abuse, and those reached by the longer access roads or located a few miles up a trail see few visitors at all.

## Access Areas

Idaho's best bubblies are found in the central mountain ranges. They're grouped here by similar road access into the seven sections shown on the locator map. These sections are defined by approach routes rather than by political or wilderness boundaries so that the greedy gourmet with limited time may sample several on the same trip.

A tiny north central area, covered in the first section of text (A), is found between Lewiston and Missoula via U.S. Highway 12. It lies along the Lochsa River in Clearwater National Forest. One of the three hot springs here is tucked away in the Selway-Bitterroot Wilderness.

The west central area, covered in the next four sections (B, C, D, E), is reached northeast of Boise by State Routes 55 and 21. In a giant nutshell, it includes all of the backcountry west of the Sawtooth crest and extends north into the southwestern quarter of the River of No Return Wilderness. Outside of the two wildlands, most of the hot soaks and hikes are found in the rolling mountains of Boise National Forest.

An east central area, covered in the final two sections (F, G), is accessed northwest of Idaho Falls by State Route 75 and U.S. Highway 93. It consists mainly of the eastern side of the Sawtooth range and the Sawtooth National Recreation Area (SNRA), plus the southeastern quarter of the River of No Return Wilderness to the north.

## Wilderness Hot Springs and Hikes

Central Idaho is composed of a mountainous mass, fully 100 miles wide and 300 miles long, etched by deep river canyons. The Selway-Bitterroot Wilderness forms the northern third of this spine, and the vast River of No Return fills in most of the remainder. The combined wildland is among the most pristine areas left in the old 48 states. Whitewater float trips are the main drawing card, and the hiking trails are scarcely touched outside of hunting season. The scenery for the most part is subtle compared to the jagged Sawtooths to the south. The canyons are dotted with sagebrush and ponderosa pine up to around 7,000 feet, while forests of spruce and fir dominate the higher elevations.

The Selway-Bitterroot Wilderness, with over 1.3 million acres, covers four national forests. From the adjacent River of No Return Wilderness to the south, it stretches north almost to U.S. Highway 12. Hikes 11a,b climb to steamy pools and remote lakes in the northwestern corner, and Hikes 13a-c lead to easy-access soaks farther east plus a dip into the wilderness just beyond.

The 2.3-million acre Frank Church-River of No Return Wilderness spreads out through six national forests and forms the largest designated wildland in the lower 48 states. Near the northern boundary, the mountains are bisected by the mighty Salmon—the legendary "River of No Return". Farther south, the 100-mile long Middle Fork Salmon River carves a deep gouge through the Salmon River Mountains.

A surprising number of virtually unknown hot springs lie concealed along the Middle Fork and its many tributaries. As the few access roads are far apart, the trips are grouped for the traveler's convenience into four separate sections. Eight of these far-flung gems may be reached by the following six hikes: 20a, 31a, 32/33a, 42a, 44a, and 45/46a. With few exceptions, they exact their toll in the form of long dusty roads and lengthy "upside-down" treks that start on top of a mountain and wind up at the bottom.

Just south of the canyon country of the River of No Return rise the alpine peaks of the Sawtooth Wilderness, filling 217,000 prime acres of the Sawtooth National Recreation Area. The Sawtooths draw hikers along 300 miles of well tended paths through an intricate landscape of colorful granite shaped into countless needle-edged spires, peaks, and ridges. Small lakes and streams are fringed with postage stamp meadows lush with wildflowers and forests of spruce, fir and pine. The area contains more than 42 peaks reaching over 10,000 feet.

Unfortunately, the Sawtooths have no hike-in hot springs. They do, however, offer several roadside ones not far from major trailheads. On the east side of the range, hot dips found in the SNRA (38-41) may be alternated with popular routes into the high country (Hikes 38a-c). On the west side, trailhead bubblies and less congested paths out of Grandjean (Hikes 30a,b) and Atlanta (Hikes 35a-c) do much to make up for the extra mileage on both tires and boots.

## Season

The climate in central Idaho is generally warmer and drier than that in the Cascades. The high Sawtooths are often obscured by snow until late July and snowed in again by mid-September. Summers are usually warm, and thunderstorms aren't uncommon. The wildlands to the north see drier and hotter weather; the hiking season lasts from early July through September and is limited chiefly by the snowpack on the high access roads. Summers west and east of the Sawtooths are longer yet, drier and pleasantly hot for the most part. Off-season access here is hampered less by foul weather than by seasonal road closures and high river levels through the spring months.

# A. OUT OF LOWELL

U.S. Highway 12 crosses north central Idaho between Lewiston, on the western edge, and Missoula, across the Montana border. It follows the Lochsa River through green forests to an area spanning the 65 miles between Lowell and Powell Junction. A quiet trail in the Selway-Bitterroot Wilderness leads to hot soaks at Stanley and continues south with a rugged backcountry loop (Hikes 11a,b). Farther up the highway, Weir Creek conceals a hidden gem. Ten miles on up the road, a path to popular Jerry Johnson dips into the wilderness beyond (Hikes 13a-c).

# 11 Stanley Hot Springs

## HIKE 11a  *To Stanley Hot Springs*

**General description:** A moderate 11-mile, round-trip day hike or overnighter featuring secluded soakers in an age-old forest, east of Lewiston in the Selway-Bitterroot Wilderness. Swimwear superfluous baggage.
**Elevation gain and loss:** +1,620 feet, -120 feet.
**Trailhead elevation:** 2,100 feet.

*This toasty pool at Stanley Hot Springs, lined with giant logs, offers the tired hiker a soothing neck massage.*

**High point:** Stanley, 3,600 feet.
**Maps:** Huckleberry Butte 7.5-minute USGS quad or Selway-Bitterroot Wilderness (Forest Service contour map); Clearwater National Forest.

**Finding the trailhead:** Drive 26 miles northeast of Lowell on U.S. Highway 12 to Wilderness Gateway Campground. Go past Loops A and B, and the amphitheater, to Trail 211 parking area. The springs are marked on the forest and USGS maps but not on the wilderness map.

**The hike:** Water steams out of a canyon bank, tumbles through a chain of delectable hot pools lined with rocks and giant logs, then continues down past the trail to the creek below. The bubblies come in all sizes and shapes and range in temperature from 90 to 110 degrees. Spacious campsites tucked into the nearby woods make this an inviting overnight stay or a good base camp for the Seven Lakes Loop (Hike 11b).

The well tended path climbs a few switchbacks and then traverses a hillside well above Boulder Creek to enter the Selway-Bitterroot Wilderness in about two miles. The elevated route provides a number of pleasant views up and down the wide valley. Bracken fern and thimbleberries line the path and cover the surrounding slopes between islands of Douglas-fir and pines.

At a signed trail junction in five miles, take the right fork (221) marked "to Maude and Lottie Lakes". The path drops downhill to cross Boulder Creek on a rustic but sturdy log pack bridge and enters a dark forest with a plush green carpet. Continue south along the edge of Huckleberry Creek and you'll find the soaking pools in a large clearing above the trail just beyond a couple of campsites.

---

# HIKE 11b  *Stanley Hot Springs to the Seven Lakes Loop*

**General description:** A rugged 18-mile, loop backpack from the hot springs to a group of lonesome lakes in the rugged backcountry of the Selway-Bitterroot Wilderness.
**Elevation gain and loss:** 3,880 feet.
**Trailhead elevation:** 3,600 feet at Stanley Hot Springs.
**High point:** 6,800 feet.
**Maps:** Same as Hike 11a plus Greenside Butte 7.5-minute USGS quad.

**Finding the trailhead:** Follow Hike 11a to Stanley Hot Springs.

**The hike:** A group of "sister" lakes clusters together in a remote neighborhood of wooded ridges and peaks at the end of a lengthy side trip from the hot springs. Included in the family are lovely-but-lonesome Lottie, misunderstood Maude (left without a name when hers was given by mistake to another), and a clinging group of spinster sisters called The Seven Lakes. They don't get much company out here and welcome overnight guests with open-meadowed arms.

To pay them a call, walk south a short distance from Stanley to a junction. Take the right fork (221), a seldom maintained path signed "to Lottie and Maude Lakes". The route zigzags south up a densely forested ridge with a

# HIKE 11a  *To Stanley Hot Springs*
# HIKE 11b  *Stanley Hot Springs to the Seven Lakes Loop*

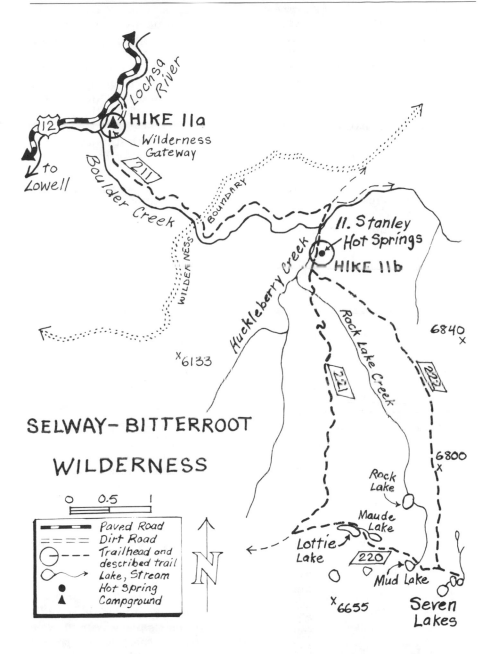

Lochsa River

HIKE 11a

Wilderness Gateway

12

to Lowell

Boulder Creek

211

WILDERNESS BOUNDARY

11. Stanley Hot Springs

HIKE 11b

Huckleberry Creek

Rock Lake Creek

6840 X

X 6133

221

222

SELWAY-BITTERROOT

WILDERNESS

6800 X

Rock Lake

Maude Lake

0  0.5  1

Lottie Lake

220

Paved Road
Dirt Road
Trailhead and described trail
Lake, Stream
Hot Spring
Campground

Mud Lake

N

X 6655

Seven Lakes

steady gain of 2,800 feet in eight miles, then drops 280 feet in the last .25 mile to a second junction.

Turn left (east) and follow a main trail (220) that skirts sky-blue Lottie Lake in .5 mile followed shortly by the real Maude Lake. The lake misnamed Maude on all the maps hides her face beneath a 6,655-foot peak south of Lottie. Climb over a low saddle to pass Mud Lake (stuck with an unenviable name) in a shallow basin off to the right. A short distance beyond the outlet comes another junction. Bear right here to reach the Seven Lakes in a total ten miles.

Two of the lakes lie alongside the trail. Low ridges and rocky knolls separate the smaller lakes and ponds in the group and conceal a variety of attractive campsites. The largest lake (at 6,484 feet) is tucked away a quarter-mile to the south. A tiny island breaks the surface, and high walls rim the southern edge of the wide basin.

For the third leg of the loop, retrace your steps to the last junction. Take the right fork (222) following a seldom used route due north. As the path climbs high above Rock Creek Canyon, the views get broader and broader. You'll pass Rock Lake 600 feet below on your left and finally reach the highest point on the hike (a crest at 6,800 feet with a 360-degree panorama of lakes and mountains) two miles above the Seven Lakes.

The path continues north and then northwest, mostly through dense woods, with a punishing plunge of 3,200 feet in the final six miles back to Stanley. Enjoy a well earned soak before retracing the 5.5 miles back to the trailhead at Wilderness Gateway Campground.

# 12 Weir Creek Hot Springs

**General description:** A quiet soaking pool cloaked in greenery at the end of a .5-mile creekside path, east of Lewiston in Clearwater National Forest. Swimwear optional. Elevation 2,900 feet.

**Directions:** Drive about 45 miles northeast of Lowell on U.S. Highway 12. Park in a pullout along the Lochsa River just east of milepost 142 at the bridge over Weir Creek. Follow a twisting and sometimes slippery path up the west side of the creek to reach the pool, staying on the route closest to the creek. The springs are marked on the forest map, but the path isn't shown.

**The hot springs:** A delightful bather-built pool, bordered by split logs, sits under a canopy of evergreens above a lively creek. The water is constantly cleaned by an ample flow from the 117-degree springs, and the temperature can be fine tuned with the aid of a removable wooden gutter. A hot springer's dream come true!

*"Key-note":* I returned to my locked car after a dip to discover the key still hanging in the ignition! No way in short of breaking a window, 80 miles from the nearest town, the sun sinking fast, and my camping gear in plain view but out of reach. Just when I'd absorbed these cold facts, a passing motorist came to the rescue. With a piece of fence wire bent into a loop, he fished for the doorlock-pull through a slit in the window while I pulled down on the glass. He managed to ring it after several misses, but the loop slid off

the slick-sided pull as soon as he tugged, thanks to modern burglarproof engineering. By this time I'd lost all hope, but not so my determined new friend. He eventually succeeded in hooking the key ring itself, maneuvered it out of the ignition, and inched it out through the slit in the window! We drank an immediate toast to success with the cold beer liberated from my cooler.

## HOT SPRINGS 12   *Weir Creek Hot Springs*

*Couples can enjoy quiet moments to themselves by the secluded pool at Weir Creek Hot Springs.*

# 13 Jerry Johnson Hot Springs

## HIKE 13a *To Jerry Johnson Hot Springs*

**General description:** An easy 2-mile, round-trip stroll to soaker-full pools in a scenic valley, east of Lewiston in Clearwater National Forest. A skinnydipper's delight.
**Elevation gain and loss:** 150 feet.
**Trailhead elevation:** 3,050 feet.
**High point:** Jerry Johnson, 3,200 feet.
**Maps:** Selway-Bitterroot Wilderness (Forest Service contour map); Clearwater National Forest.

**Finding the trailhead:** Take U.S. Highway 12 about 55 miles northeast of Lowell (or 10.5 miles southwest of Powell junction) to Warm Springs Pack Bridge, which spans the Lochsa River .5 mile west of milepost 152. There's ample parking nearby, and the trail sign is across the bridge. The springs are marked on the forest map but not on the wilderness map.

**The hike:** Three separate hot springs, each with two or more soaking pools, lie near a creek in a broad valley forested with tall stands of old-growth cedar and Grand fir. Spacious campsites are scattered in the surrounding woods, but due to the year around popularity of the springs, vandalism has become a problem that may force the Forest Service to ban overnight camping.

Turn right across the pack bridge onto Warm Springs Creek Trail (49). Follow the forested path along the creek for an easygoing mile upvalley. The first two rock-lined soakers are down at the water line and are easy to miss if unoccupied; at 115 degrees, they need a creek water mix to drop into the comfort zone. You can't miss the second group of shallow pools. They cross the trail in a chain leading down to the creek-each slightly cooler than the one above.

The third spring, a short way beyond the others in a grassy meadow above the trail, has two rock and mud soaking pools. One of them is over knee-deep and large enough to float several cozy bodies; it maintains a steady 106 degrees without a mix from the creek. However, the silty bottom is easily stirred up—if you plan on climbing out clean, you'll have to find some means of doing it without standing up. Lots of luck!

*The upper spring at Jerry Johnson trickles into a scenic pool well above the creek.*

# HIKE 13b  *Jerry Johnson Hot Springs to The Falls*

**General description:** A moderate 5-mile, round-trip day hike from the hot springs up the creek canyon on a quiet trail in Clearwater National Forest.
**Elevation gain and loss:** 800 feet.
**Trailhead elevation:** 3,200 feet at the hot springs.
**High point:** The Falls, 4,000 feet.
**Maps:** Same as Hike 13a.

**Finding the trailhead:** Follow Hike 13a to Jerry Johnson.

**The hike:** The valley bordering Warm Springs Creek rises to a modest overlook. The Falls are a chain of small dropoffs and pools—don't expect a classic waterfall. The view from the trail is obscured by trees and too distant to be impressive, but the route up the canyon is a pleasant climb through old-growth woods.

Stroll a mile south from the hot springs on Warm Springs Creek Trail past a junction with a trail branching off to the right (Hike 13c). Beyond this point the valley begins to narrow and steepen, and the path switchbacks well above the east bank through deep forest. A brief detour up and around one major side canyon adds a little variety. You'll reach the best overlook of the falls about .25 mile beyond the wilderness marker.

# HIKE 13c  *Jerry Johnson Hot Springs to Bear Mountain*

**General description:** A strenuous 12-mile, round-trip day hike or overnighter from the hot springs to a mountaintop overlooking the Selway-Bitterroot Wilderness.
**Elevation gain and loss:** +4,160 feet, -200 feet.
**Trailhead elevation:** 3,200 feet at the hot springs.
**High point:** Bear Mountain Lookout, 7,184 feet.
**Maps:** Same as Hike 13a, or Bear Mountain and Tom Beal Peak 7.5-minute USGS quads.

**Finding the trailhead:** Follow Hike 13a to Jerry Johnson.

**The hike:** A bird's-eye view of the Lochsa River canyon to the north and the Selway-Bitterroot Wilderness backcountry to the south is the reward for a nonstop uphill grind to the lookout tower capping Bear Mountain.

From the hot springs, walk a mile south up the wide valley on Warm Springs Creek Trail to a signed junction with McConnell Mountain Trail (213). (Bear Mountain is just the first stop on this route—the trail shoots up just below the summit on its way south to 240-foot higher McConnell Mountain.)

Turn west on this path and cross a pack bridge spanning Warm Springs Creek. Zigzag upward through thick forest and trudge southwest up the seemingly endless ridge above Queen Creek. The route contours south around an

*The trail to Jerry Johnson winds through a forest of old-crowth cedar and Grand fir.*

unnamed peak and then follows the wilderness boundary westward. It finally dips across a rocky saddle and rises to a junction at 7,000 feet just below the summit.

McConnell Mountain Trail drops south at this point, and a .5-mile spur covers the final, tapering stretch to the summit. There's a campsite near the junction, and a short path leads from the lookout spur to a spring with good water on the west side of Bear Mountain.

*A short side trip from Jerry Johnson follows the creek to a series of drop-offs called the Falls.*

# HIKE 13a  *To Jerry Johnson Hot Springs*
# HIKE 13b  *Jerry Johnson Hot Springs to The Falls*
# HIKE 13c  *Jerry Johnson Hot Springs to Bear Mountain*

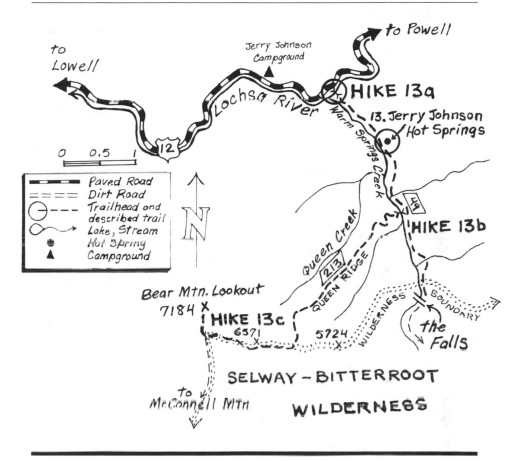

to Powell

Jerry Johnson
Campground

to
Lowell

Lochsa River

HIKE 13a

13. Jerry Johnson
Hot Springs

Warm Springs Creek

0    0.5    1

12

**Paved Road**
**Dirt Road**
**Trailhead and**
**described trail**
**Lake, Stream**
**Hot Spring**
**Campground**

N

49

HIKE 13b

Queen Creek

213

QUEEN RIDGE

WILDERNESS

BOUNDARY

Bear Mtn. Lookout
7184 X

HIKE 13c
6571          5724

the
Falls

To
McConnell Mtn

SELWAY – BITTERROOT

WILDERNESS

# B. OUT OF CASCADE & WARM LAKE

North of Boise, a forest highway runs northeast from State Route 55 at Cascade to intersect a dirt road leading to hot dips along the South Fork Salmon River (14-18) and a couple of trails (Hikes 17a,18a) in the Warm Lake area of Boise Forest. Next, the road follows the river north into Payette National Forest to a hot pool hidden at Mile-16 and a nearby trailhead (Hikes 19a,b). Northeast of this area, a mad expedition into the River of No Return Wilderness ends at Kwiskwis Hot Spring (Hike 20a).

# 14 Trail Creek Hot Spring

**General description:** Peekaboo pools and a bathtub in a wooded canyon below a highway, northeast of Cascade in Boise National Forest. Keep cutoffs handy. Elevation 5,900 feet.

**Directions:** From State Route 55 at Cascade, take the paved Warm Lake Road about 19 miles northeast. Watch for a large pullout on your right at .4 mile east of milepost 61. Slide down a slippery 60-yard path from the west end to the canyon floor and up Trail Creek to the soaking pools. The spring isn't marked on the forest map.

**The hot spring:** A 115-degree spring spreads rivulets down a creek bank into a few shallow pools. Between them perches a bathtub filled with steaming water fed in by a hose. The temperature can be lowered by adding creek water, and a handy bucket (sometimes) sits nearby. The spot is visible from the west side of the pullout but just out of sight from passing motorists.

# 15 Molly's Tubs

**General description:** A bevy of bathtubs on the South Fork Salmon River hidden below a dirt road, northeast of Cascade in Boise National Forest. A swimsuit/birthday suit mix. Elevation 5,200 feet.

**Directions:** From State Route 55 at Cascade, take the paved Warm Lake Road about 23 miles northeast (3.7 miles past Trail Creek Hot Spring) to graded Forest Road 474. Drive south for 1.3 miles to a small pullout on your right and follow a short path down to the tubs. The spring isn't shown on the forest map.

**The hot spring:** Five brightly painted bathtubs lined up side by side, plus three more sitting just below, collect the flow from this spring with the aid of hoses which the user can move from one to another. River water may be added for a cooler soak. Beside the tubs are a wooden bench and a homemade

*Trail Creek Hot Spring has acquired a bathtub set between the creekside pools. It's a welcome addition and hopefully will survive spring runoffs.*

clothes rack—all sitting on raised platforms that span the muddy channel running from the spring to the nearby river. How civilized can a primitive hot spring get?

# 16 Molly's Hot Spring

**General description:** A soaker-friendly pool above the South Fork Salmon River located .25 mile from a dirt road, northeast of Cascade in Boise National Forest. Bathing suits optional. Elevation 5,300 feet.

**Directions:** Follow the directions above to Forest Road 474 and go south 1.9 miles (.6 mile past Molly's Tubs) to a junction. Park here and walk west on a road closed to motor vehicles that leads to the river and soon bridges it. Immediately past the bridge, hang a right on an overgrown path that meanders back downstream and up a short slope to the pool. Molly's isn't marked on the forest map.

**The hot spring:** A wall of trees stands guard over a 120-degree spring tumbling down a slope above the river. The square soaking pool built in the center of the steamy flow is lined with plastic held in place by poles shaped from lodgepole pines. Good circulation keeps it clean, and the temperature can be lowered by diverting the incoming hoses. A hand-lettered sign nailed to a nearby tree proclaims "Duke's Hot Spring", but it's better known as Molly's. There's a plywood platform to dry off on and a view through the trees of the river below.

*Molly's "short cut":* While enjoying a pleasant soak, I was joined by a friendly young couple. In the course of conversation, it turned out that the lady was a professional barber who just happened to have all the tools of her trade in their camper! An hour later, wrapped in a plastic apron with a towel around my neck, shears clicking and hair flying to the winds, I sat on a handy stump at their camp in a nearby meadow while she treated me to an expert trim.

*Molly's Tubs, at last count, had five new bathtubs in addition to the three shown here.*

# HOT SPRING 14 *Trail Creek Hot Spring*
# HOT SPRINGS 15 *Molly's Tubs*
# HOT SPRINGS 16 *Molly's Hot Spring*

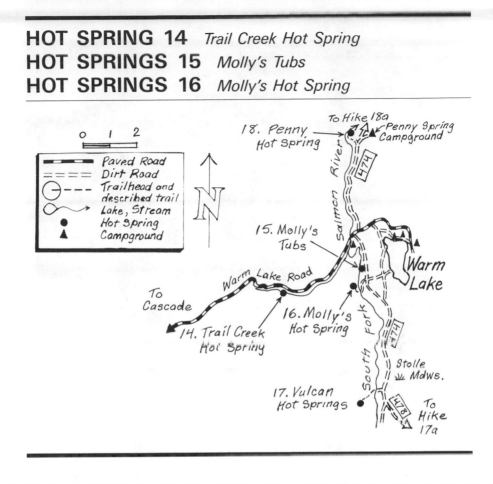

*The hot spring that fills the pool at Molly's was once used to supply a nearby swimming pool, now in ruins, called the South Fork Plunge.*

# 17 Vulcan Hot Springs

**General description:** A popular creek-wide soaker at the end of a .5-mile path, northeast of Cascade in Boise National Forest. Swimwear optional despite heavy use. Elevation 5,600 feet.

**Directions:** Follow the directions to Forest Road 474 given in 15. Drive south about 6.5 miles (4.6 miles past Molly's and shortly beyond Stolle Meadows). A spur on your right ends at an unofficial camping area by the river and a split-log footbridge at the trailhead. The unsigned path crosses two more logs and soon reaches a creek littered with fallen trees, then follows the warming stream uphill to the pool. Just beyond lies the spectacular source of the now-steaming creek. Vulcan is named on the forest map.

**The hot springs:** Many bubbling springs join forces to form a hot creek which cools as it flows down a wooded hillside toward the South Fork Salmon River. The creek has been dammed with logs at the point of optimum soaking temperature (around 105 degrees) to form an emerald-green soaking pool about 30 feet across with a sand and mud bottom. This is a heavily used spot that shows some signs of abuse. Please treat it with care.

# HIKE 17a  *Rice Peak*

**General description:** A strenuous 4-mile, round-trip day climb to a peak in Boise National Forest with distant views, near Vulcan Hot Springs.

**Elevation gain and loss:** 1,580 feet.

**Trailhead elevation:** 7,120 feet.

**High point:** Rice Peak Lookout, 8,700 feet.

**Maps:** Warm Lake 15-minute USGS quad; Boise National Forest.

**Finding the trailhead:** Follow the road access above to Vulcan. Continue south for just under a mile and bear left on Rice Peak Road (Forest Road 478). The 6-mile road gradually deteriorates, and you may be better off walking the final 2-mile stretch unless you have a 4WD. Check with the ranger in Cascade for current conditions; mud often makes access impossible before July. If you hike the last two miles up Rice Creek to the trailhead, you can tack on an extra 800-foot gain. The trail is marked on the forest map but not on the old USGS quad.

**The hike:** Warm Lake is a better area for geothermal gems than for interesting hikes, the climb to Rice Peak being one of the few exceptions. The 360-degree view from the lookout reveals an expanse of distant peaks ranging from the Salmon River Mountains to the double silhouette of the Sawtooths backed by the White Clouds, around to the wooded mountains above Cascade and McCall.

Rice Peak trail (103) continues up Rice Creek where the road leaves off and reaches tiny Rice Lake in .5 mile. Cross the outlet on logs and circle the north shore past some grassy campsites. Now the path climbs a long, steep mile to

*The steamy pool at Vulcan seems to be getting a tad hotter every year. If this trend keeps up, a new soaker may have to be built somewhere downstream.*

a saddle just south of the peak, takes a short break, then zigzags up the last .5 mile to the summit. On the return trip, many hikers take a short cut by boulder hopping straight down the west side of the mountain to Rice Lake.

# HOT SPRINGS 17  *Vulcan Hot Springs*
# HIKE 17a  *Rice Peak*

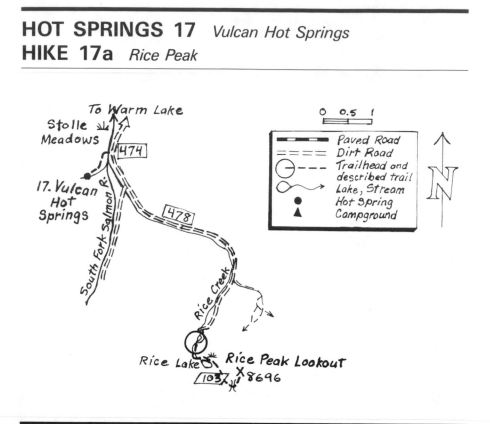

# 18 Penny Hot Spring

**General description:** A lonesome spring in the South Fork Salmon River Canyon reached by a .5-mile path, northeast of Cascade in Boise National Forest. Naked bodies welcome. Elevation 4,800 feet.

**Directions:** Follow the directions to Forest Road 474 given in 15. Drive 4.4 miles north, then turn left just past the Nickel Creek sign near Penny Spring Campground. The overgrown road soon transforms into a path that shows more sign of deerprints than footprints. The route curves north around a hill above the river, then drops sharply beside a cliff to the pools at the bottom. The spring isn't marked on the forest map.

**The hot spring:** Steaming water flows down the side of a cliff into a few rock and sand pools along a scenic bend in the river. (You can spot several other hot springs on the opposite bank by the telltale orange slime). Penny gets very little use or upkeep, and the fragile pools swamp during high water. There's plenty of hot water just waiting for some energetic soul to rebuild a proper soaking pool, so if you're intent on a bath, bring a shovel and plenty of elbow grease!

For "what it's worth", the road from Warm Lake to Penny Hot Spring passes Two-bit and Six-bit Creeks on one side, then Dime and Nickel Creeks on the other. Dollar Creek lies just beyond (see Hike 18a). To sum it up: A penny's just a penny, but this one's got potential.

*At Penny Hot Spring, river water at your elbow can be channeled into the pools to produce whatever temperature you prefer.*

# HIKE 18a *Needles Junction*

**General description:** A moderate 16-mile, round-trip day hike or overnighter along a ridge in the northwest corner of Boise National Forest, near Penny Hot Spring.

**Elevation gain and loss:** +3,180 feet, -840 feet.

**Trailhead elevation:** 4,920 feet.

**High point:** Needles Junction, 7,218 feet.

**Maps:** Warm Lake and Gold Fork 15-minute USGS quads; Boise National Forest.

**Finding the trailhead:** Follow the road access above to Penny. Continue north about a mile past the campground and turn left at 5.5 miles across a river bridge. Take the next left (Forest Road 493) and bump a short way uphill to a small trail sign and pullout.

**The hike:** This quiet trail in a lightly used part of the forest offers modest views across green valleys to rolling mountain ranges and a few isolated peaks. Outlooks near the Needles Junction reveal two sharp spires of Gold Fork Rock to the southwest and an 8,300-foot upthrust of rocky turrets to the northwest known as The Needles.

Dollar Creek Ridge Trail (14) zigzags 2,040 uphill feet, curving westward through a recent burn to crest at about 4.5 miles. The route then dips and rises in a swing to the northwest, dropping off 140 feet in the 2-mile stretch down to Dollar Creek. An unmaintained path branches off to the right and leads back to the trailhead above the north bank.

The path crosses Dollar Creek and shoots up 900 feet in 1.5 miles to reach the high point on the trip, the Needles Junction, at 7,218 feet. The trail is bisected here by another ridgeline path, the Needles Route. For better views, go north on this trail for .5 mile. The junction is a good spot to catch your breath and enjoy the scenery before heading back down the ridge or on to more distant horizons. There's a good campsite near a creek at the junction.

# HOT SPRING 18 *Penny Hot Spring*
# HIKE 18a *Needles Junction*

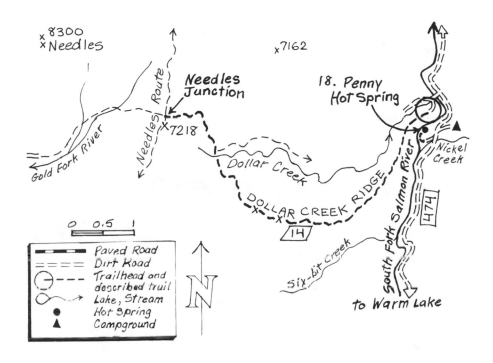

# 19 Mile-16 Hot Spring

**General description:** A sylvan soaker in the South Fork Salmon River Canyon hidden below a dirt road, northeast of Cascade in Payette National Forest. Highly skinnydippable. Elevation 4,150 feet.

**Directions:** Follow the directions to Forest Road 474 given in 15. Drive north about 14.5 dusty miles to Poverty Flat Campground, the trailhead for the following two hikes. Go 1.6 miles farther and park as close as you can to the edge. Don't depend on spotting the milepost-16 marker; it has a strange tendency to vanish no matter how often it's replaced! There are no landmarks to go by— not even a proper pullout marks the spot. Hunt for a path dropping over the steep bank to the pool. Mile-16 isn't marked on the forest map.

**The hot spring:** A crystal-clear soaking pool, well concealed from the nearby road, sits at the base of a steep bank on the river's edge. It's enclosed by attractive chunks of stream rock mortared tightly in place. A large slab at one end makes a perfect backrest for enjoying the view up the tree-studded canyon. Spring water, cooling from 115 degrees as it trickles down the bank, can be diverted by means of a long pipe coupled to a hose, and the temperature seems to stay a steady perfect.

Referred to locally as Mile-16 Hot Spring because of its strategic location on the road, it's also known as Fire Crew and Holdover. Whatever it's called, this is a top notch, tastefully designed pool in a great setting. Please don't abuse the privilege of using it—remember, no soap or shampoo.

# HIKE 19a  *Blackmare Lake*

**General description:** A moderate 18-mile, round-trip overnighter to a remote lake in Payette National Forest, near Mile-16 Hot Spring.
**Elevation gain and loss:** +3,100 feet, -500 feet.
**Trailhead elevation:** 4,200 feet.
**High point:** Blackmare Lake, 7,040 feet.

*This 5-star delight at Mile-16 Hot Spring is a prime example of how to design and build a proper soaking pool.*

**Maps:** Blackmare and White Rock Peak 7.5-minute USGS quads; Payette National Forest.

**Finding the trailhead:** Follow the directions above to Poverty Flat Campground and park at the south end by the pack bridge. Cross the South Fork Salmon River to the trail sign for both Blackmare Lake and White Rock Peak.

**The hike:** Sapphire-blue Blackmare Lake, lying in a basin flanked by granite walls, makes a pleasant overnight trip. Half a dozen 8,000-foot peaks rim the basin, and narrow bands of trees mark the ridges with diagonal stripes. The isolated lake nestles at the head of a long glacial valley that provides access for the lightly used trail.

Turn right across the bridge onto Blackmare Trail (100). You can count on wet feet fording Blackmare Creek (which could be treacherous during high water). The wooded route then climbs well above the north bank and follows the creek westward up the steep-walled valley. At a branch in the trail in just under four miles, bear left a short distance downhill to a second junction.

Take the right fork southwest along the South Fork of Blackmare Creek (302). This stretch has a fairly even and gentle grade. After crossing a few side streams and then the creek itself, you'll pass the South Fork Cutoff in seven miles. Turn back across the creek and climb 1,360 feet in the final 2-mile stretch upvalley to Blackmare Lake.

---

# HIKE 19b   *White Rock Peak*

**General description:** A strenuous 10-mile, round-trip day climb to a mountaintop in Payette National Forest, near Mile-16 Hot Spring.
**Elevation gain and loss:** 3,575 feet.
**Trailhead elevation:** 4,200 feet.
**High point:** White Rock Peak, 7,775 feet.
**Maps:** White Rock Peak 7.5-minute USGS quad; Payette National Forest.

**Finding the trailhead:** Follow the road access for Hike 19a.

**The hike:** If you're more in the mood for a backbreaking climb than a creekside stroll, this scramble up a seldom used trail will fit the bill! There are glimpses between trees of the surrounding hills as you climb the ridge and a modest view from the summit.

Turn left across the bridge onto White Rock Peak Trail (303). Switchbacks drag the rough path southwestward up the ridge through a forest of pine and Douglas-fir to reach the summit in five grueling miles. Watch your footing-the track is eroded and slippery in many spots. Be sure to drop in for a relaxing soak at "Mile-16" after the hike.

# HOT SPRING 19 *Mile-16 Hot Spring*
# HIKE 19a *Blackmare Lake*
# HIKE 19b *White Rock Peak*

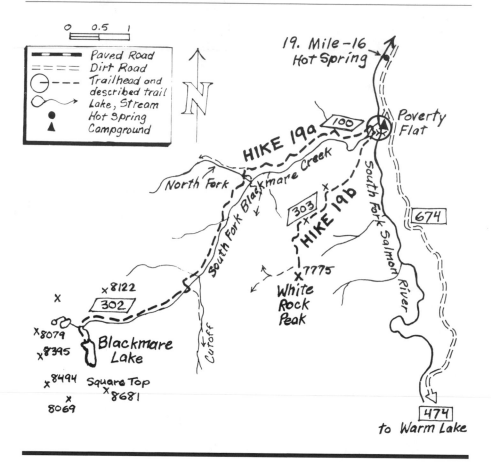

# 20 Kwiskwis Hot Spring

## HIKE 20a  To Kwiskwis Hot Spring

**General description:** A wild and woolly 13-mile, round-trip day hike or over-nighter to an isolated hot spring on a creek above the Middle Fork Salmon River, buried in the River of No Return Wilderness southeast of Yellow Pine. Swimwear totally nonfunctional here except for sun protection factor.
**Elevation gain and loss:** +340 feet, -2,780 feet.
**High point:** Trailhead, 8,120 feet.
**Low point:** Kwiskwis, 5,680 feet.
**Maps:** Big Chief Creek and Big Baldy 7.5-minute USGS quads, or River of No Return Wilderness, South half (Forest Service contour map); Challis National Forest.

**Warning:** This somewhat crazy expedition is for hardcore wilderness buffs and hot springs fanatics only! The obscure trailhead at Mule Hill, on the brink of the vast River of No Return Wilderness, is over 70 miles from the nearest paved road back at Warm Lake. The final 23 teeth-jarring miles of corrugated and rocky dirt from the closest town, Yellow Pine, are enough to test the mettle of the most determined adventurer (not to mention his or her vehicle). The primitive trail plunges downhill to a creek valley that reaches a hot spring few folks have ever heard of and fewer still have ever visited.

If you decide to brave the trip in, you'll be rewarded with views of undulating mountains and gentle valleys, acres of solitude in a lovely creekside meadow with idyllic camping, and a money-back guarantee that you won't have to wait in line for a soak at Kwiskwis Hot Spring.

**Finding the trailhead:** Follow the directions to Forest Road 474 given in 15 and drive north about 34 dusty miles to the upper end. Turn right on Forest Road 48 and proceed 15 even dustier miles to Yellow Pine. (Last chance to buy gas—or anything else!) Check with the sheriff on the status of Meadow Creek Lookout Road. Continue the grind east for 14 miles on Forest Road 412, an active mining road, to an eye-catching 4-way stop sign at Stibnite.

A tiny gold mining settlement during the 1930s, Stibnite mushroomed to a population of over a thousand during World War II when it became the country's biggest producer of tungsten. When the war boom ended, it dwindled into a ghost town. But Stibnite has recently sprung back to life once again as the home of an ambitious new gold mining venture.

Climb five rocky and serpentine miles on Forest Road 375 to Monumental Summit (open from July 1 to November 15) and watch for a primitive road (641) signed "to Meadow Creek Lookout" dropping off to your right. The narrowing ridge road winds out to the trailhead on Mule Hill. Drivers of low clearance vehicles will have to skirt a few rocks (if the width of the road allows) or stop to toss them over the edge, but the road is usually passable.

Keep your eyes peeled in four miles for signs of an old horse camp in a clearing on the ridgetop. This is the "certified trailhead" at 8,120 feet. Park here and walk back up the road to the woods. Search for U.S. Forest Service

Trail 219 on your right (south), and you'll find an overgrown path marked by a faded sign that simply says "Primitive Area." This is it—last chance to change your mind!

**The hike:** The track drops southeast down the flank of Mule Hill, passes the crumbling remains of an old log cabin, then plunges in earnest southward down a twisting ridge. In one or two places it snakes down sloping meadows with wall-to-wall views, but for most of the 2.5-mile, 2,000-foot drop, the route is engulfed in virgin forest.

The path finally comes to rest in a peaceful valley at the junction of Indian Creek Trail (225). The creek flows southeast to join the Middle Fork Salmon River in about 15 miles; Kwiskwis, named on all the maps, lies four miles downstream. You'll soon reach broad Kiwah Meadow—a delightful spot to

*Kwiskwis Hot Spring spreads out a feast of hot water and Indian Creek supplies the cold. The rare guest must furnish the only thing missing—a proper soaking pool.*

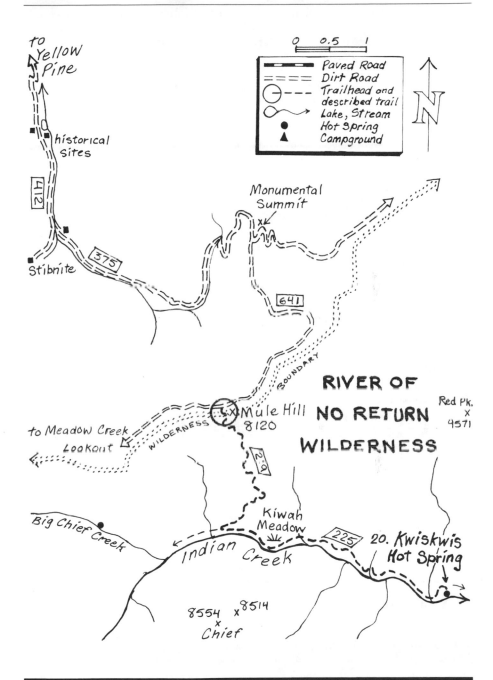

settle down for a lunch break or a week's retreat from the cares of the world. The path is hard to see through the knee-high grass but picks up again beyond this point.

After crossing the first side creek, the route climbs high up the north bank to traverse a precipitous talus slope. It's hard to be sure of the "official" trail as there are a maze of game paths crisscrossing at varying heights. Most are badly eroded and hard to cling to but all lead in the same direction— downstream. You'll know you're on the right track at the third stream crossing (Kwiskwis Creek) if you see a faded sign that labels it "Quis Quis". A short way beyond, you should intersect the upper springs.

Scalding water emerges from the ground at temperatures up to 156 degrees but drops into the comfort zone by the time it reaches Indian Creek below. More springs appear as you follow the broad flow downhill. The shallow pool(s) at the bottom fill in with creek gravel and will need some excavation work, but that's just the price you pay for "the wilderness experience" and a steamy soak at the end of the trail. There's a small campsite across the creek, but the best camping by far is back at Kiwah Meadow.

An element adding even more spice to the adventure is the fact that the Forest Service has little firsthand information to help the hiker. This remote area is a slice of the Frank Church-River of No Return "wilderness pie" held by Boise National Forest but administered, at least in theory, by Challis National Forest. However, the District Office sits roughly 70 air miles across the state map from Mule Hill.

By a series of roundabout roads, a trail crew based in Challis would have to drive a staggering 180 miles to reach the trailhead, and only 80 of them would be on pavement. The final hundred miles of dirt get progressively worse over potholes and rock. As a result, this is one piece of wilderness that seems more than likely to remain just that!

# C. OUT OF CROUCH

Midway between Boise and Cascade and just east of State Route 55 is the tiny town of Crouch. A dirt road in Boise National Forest follows the Middle Fork Payette River northeast of town. The scenic canyon contains all of the hot springs in this small but fertile area. Three roadside dips (21-23) are followed by a series accessed by a river trail. Moondipper and Pine Burl (Hike 24/25a) are the best of the bunch.

# 21 Rocky Canyon Hot Spring

**General description:** Highly visible hot pools on the wrong side of the Middle Fork Payette River, northeast of Crouch in Boise National Forest. Swimwear essential. Elevation 3,440 feet.

**Directions:** From State Route 55 at Banks, take the Garden Valley Road about

*To reach Rocky Canyon Hot Spring, the user must ford the river and scramble up the opposite bank.*

10 paved miles east to Crouch. Follow graded Forest Road 698 northeast about 12.5 miles (1.5 miles past Hardscrabble Campground) and park in a pullout on your left. You'll have to wade the wide river, which could be dangerous during high water. The spring is marked on the forest map.

**The hot spring:** Near the mouth of Rocky Canyon, a spring flows at 120 degrees down a slope to the river. Bathers have carved out a few small pools dropping step-by-step down the rocky ledges, and each pool is slightly cooler than the one above. Take your pick!

# 22 Fire Crew Hot Spring

**General description:** Roadside hot dips screened by woods on the Middle Fork Payette River, northeast of Crouch in Boise National Forest. Keep cutoffs handy. Elevation 3,600 feet.

**Directions:** Follow the directions above to Forest Road 698. Drive about 15 dusty miles (2.5 miles past Rocky Canyon Hot Spring) to a junction at Trail Creek Campground. Take the left fork (still 698) for .3 mile, then bear left on a spur ending at the river. A loop encircles an unofficial camping area; the pools are out on a gravel bar to your right. Fire Crew isn't shown on the forest map.

*The water-level pools at Fire Crew Hot Spring are swamped in the spring runoff and landlocked by midsummer.*

**The hot spring:** A few pools framed by sun-warmed rocks are concealed from the road just upstream from Rocky Canyon. Also at the river's edge but luckily on the near side, these little known dips are frequented chiefly by (you guessed it) the local fire crew. Early in the season, the hot flow through the pools can be fine tuned by adjusting a rock or two around the edges. It's an attractive spot and sometimes a pleasant surprise.

# 23 Boiling Springs

**General description:** Easy-access hot springs and soaks on the Middle Fork Payette River, northeast of Crouch in Boise National Forest. Nudity a no-no if you're over five. Elevation 4,000 feet.

**Directions:** Follow the directions to Forest Road 698 given in 21. Drive about 23 miles (past Rocky Canyon and Fire Crew Hot Springs) to the road-end campground and trailhead (see Hikes 24/25a and 26a). Stroll .25 mile north to the old guard station cabin. Boiling Springs is named on the forest map.

**The hot springs:** Steaming water emerges at over 130 degrees from fissures in a cliff at Boiling Springs Guard Station and flows through a small pool hidden halfway up the rocks. The water gradually cools as it runs through a ditch across a wide meadow. A few rock-lined pools at the river's edge are usually filled on weekends with kids from the nearby campground. River water can be added for a cooler soak.

*This tiny pool at Boiling Springs, hidden between boulders just below the source, is far too hot for soaking*

# HOT SPRING 21 *Rocky Canyon Hot Spring*
# HOT SPRING 22 *Fire Crew Hot Spring*
# HOT SPRINGS 23 *Boiling Springs*

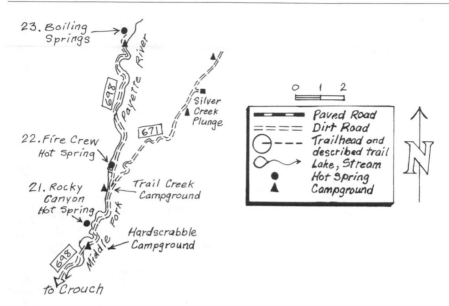

# 24/25 Moondipper and Pine Burl Hot Springs

## HIKE 24/25a *To Moondipper and Pine Burl Hot Springs*

**General description:** An easy 4-mile, round-trip double feature not to be missed, playing near the Middle Fork Payette River northeast of Crouch. A bathing suit/birthday suit mix.
**Elevation gain and loss:** 80 feet.
**Trailhead elevation:** 4,000 feet.
**High point:** Hot springs, 4,080 feet.
**Maps:** Boiling Springs 15-minute USGS quad; Boise National Forest.

**Finding the trailhead:** Follow the directions above to Boiling Springs and take your pick of two routes upstream. The springs are marked but not named on both maps.

**The hike:** Moondipper and Pine Burl enjoy a setting worthy of their captivating names. Two separate springs checking in at 120 degrees flow down the banks of a creek just above the river into a pair of scenic soakers spaced 200 yards apart along the tree-studded canyon. Both get swamped during high water, but are well worth a bit of annual maintenance.

An unmarked path, steep and slippery in spots, hugs the west side of the river all the way; this is the safer route when the water level is high (usually until August). The Middle Fork Trail (33) is more direct, but you'll have to ford twice in the 2-mile hike upstream. If in doubt, check with the ranger at Garden Valley.

When you reach Dash Creek, the first side stream on the west side, you'll soon find Moondipper spread out against a rocky bank. The large, sandy-

*The soaking pool at Moondipper requires some remodeling every year, but the setting makes up for the effort.*

bottomed pool can hold quite a few happy soakers and offers a lovely view up the canyon. It's usually landlocked by midsummer and can get a mite too hot for comfort by then without some means of transporting cold water from the creek.

Pine Burl, a tiny gem tucked out of sight just a few bends upstream, is a hot springer's fantasy of the perfect spot for a quiet party for two. The name is proudly inscribed, along with those of its four volunteer builders, on a small masonry dam at the downstream end. If the water gets too hot, the rocks at the other end can be shifted to let creek water trickle in.

There's a beautiful swimming hole in the river just upstream from Dash Creek, and a third tiny spring bubbles away a short way downstream. A scramble up the south bank of the creek reaches a campsite with a view on top of the ridge. If all this isn't enough to satisfy you, there are several more hot springs (though none comparable with these two) along the river's edge upstream. See Hike 26a below.

# 26 Bull Creek Hot Springs

## HIKE 26a  To Bull Creek Hot Springs

**General description:** A slightly insane 22-mile, round-trip backpack up the Middle Fork Payette River to a far-flung hot dip on Bull Creek. No need whatsoever to pack a swimsuit.
**Elevation gain and loss:** 1,200 feet.
**Trailhead elevation:** 4,000 feet.
**High point:** Bull Creek Hot Springs, 5,200 feet.
**Maps:** Same as Hike 24/25a.

**Finding the trailhead:** Follow the directions above to Boiling Springs. The springs are named on both maps.

**The hike:** The remote springs overlooking Bull Creek may or may not have a bather-friendly pool to greet you just when you really need a hot soak. Too late in the season, when a nearby side creek dries up, the stranded pool(s) grow hot enough to boil eggs and hikers alike; too early, you'll freeze more than your toes in the cold river en route. This venture would be sheer madness when the water level is high; be sure to check with the ranger at Garden Valley before setting off.

The trip combines the 2-mile stroll to Moondipper and Pine Burl (Hike 24/25a) with a 9-mile extension upstream to reach Bull Creek Hot Springs in a total of 11 miles. The path snakes back and forth across the swift-moving Middle Fork Payette River an exhausting total of twelve times en route to Bull Creek. See Hike 24/25a for a choice of routes from the trailhead to Dash Creek.

Immediately after passing Moondipper at two miles, the Middle Fork Trail (33) begins crossing the wide stream at almost every bend in its convoluted course. In the next few miles, you'll pass several minor hot springs and seeps marked on the maps. The condition of whatever pools they may have depends

*Pine Burl Hot Spring perks up through the sandy bottom of this user-built pool.*

on how many flocks of sheep have plodded through them en route to or from their summer pastures. One local ranger calls them all "hog wallows", but he's obviously not a true fanatic dedicated to the cause of investigating every hot puddle no matter how remote. Unlike some of us, he's a man of common sense!

The route climbs briefly away from the river, then continues up the west bank for a mile or so. Two more wet fords and you'll reach a welcome camping area near the mouth of Bull Creek at 7.5 miles, 4,400 feet. Best to camp here— there aren't any good campsites at the hot springs.

Wade the Middle Fork one last time to pick up Bull Creek Trail (102) on the north bank of the creek. Follow the faintly-blazed path 3.5 miles east to find the hot springs on a bluff near a small stream. See Hike 26b below for a much less difficult route from a different direction.

# HIKE 26b  *Bull Creek Hot Springs via Silver Creek Trail*

**General description:** A relatively easy 18-mile, round-trip backpack to the bubblies on Bull Creek from an alternate trailhead.
**Elevation gain and loss:** +1,540 feet, -1,280 feet.
**Trailhead elevation:** 4,940 feet.
**High point:** Silver Creek Summit, 6,240 feet.
**Maps:** Boiling Springs and Deadwood Reservoir 15-minute USGS quads; Boise National Forest.

**Finding the trailhead:** Follow the directions to Trail Creek Campground given

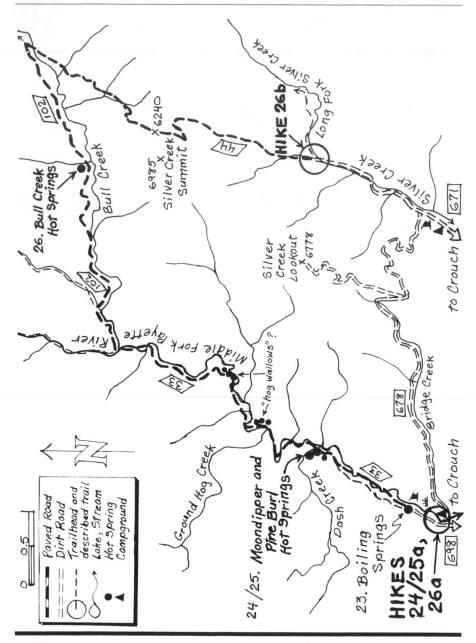

102

Silver Creek

X 6240

6985
X
Silver Creek
Summit

44

Long Fork Silver Creek

HIKE 26b

26. Bull Creek
Hot Springs

Bull Creek

Silver Creek

X 6778
Lookout

Silver Creek

671

to Crouch

102

Middle Fork Payette River

33

"hog wallows"?

678

Bridge Creek

to Crouch

N

Ground Hog Creek

Dash Creek

33

23. Boiling Springs

698

to Crouch

24/25. Moondipper and
Pine Burl
Hot Springs

**HIKES
24/25a,
26a**

Paved Road
Dirt Road
Trailhead and
described trail
Lake, Stream
Hot Spring
Campground

0  .5  1

in 22. Bear right on Silver Creek Road (Forest Road 671) and drive to the road-end parking area and trail sign (about two miles beyond the guard station).

**The hike:** Silver Creek Trail offers a far drier, more scenic, and slightly shorter approach to Bull Creek than the wet trek up the Middle Fork described above—minus the hot springs en route. See the preceding hikes for comparison and 26a for a description of Bull Creek Hot Springs. You'll gain an extra 1,300 feet climbing over Silver Creek Summit, but the views along the trail make up for it.

Two trails begin here. Be sure to take Silver Creek Trail (44) and not the one branching off to your right. Follow the route up over Silver Creek Summit at 6,240 feet, enjoy the broad views and maybe a nice dry lunch, then drop down the far side to reach Bull Creek in about six miles—a pleasant spot to spend the night.

Cross the creek and watch for the Bull Creek Trail (102) in about .25 mile. Turn left onto the blazed path and follow it three miles downstream above the north bank of Bull Creek to reach the hot springs (at 5,200 feet) on a bluff overlooking the canyon.

# D. OUT OF LOWMAN

State Route 21, the Ponderosa Pine Scenic Route, runs northeast of Boise to easy-access soaks on the South Fork Payette River at Pine Flats and Kirkham, near the tiny town of Lowman, and on to a gem at Bonneville; these dips combine well with a trek to Red Mountain and points beyond (Hikes 28a,b). Next, Sacajawea's roadside hot pools mark the Grandjean trailhead into the western Sawtooths (Hikes 30a,b). Finally, bubbles hidden in the River of No Return Wilderness to the north are reached by following Hikes 31a to Bear Valley Hot Springs and 32/33a down the Middle Fork Salmon River to Trail Flat and Sheepeater.

# 27 Pine Flats Hot Spring

**General description:** Hot dips and a built-in cliffside shower on the South Fork Payette River, west of Lowman in Boise National Forest. Bathing suits surprisingly common here. Elevation 3,700 feet.

**Directions:** From Boise, take State Route 21 about 70 miles northeast to Lowman. Turn left on the graded road to Garden Valley and drive 5 miles to Pine Flats Campground. From the west end, follow an unmarked path .3-mile downstream to a wide gravel bar; look for the hottest pool up the rocky cliff. The spring isn't marked on the forest map.

**The hot spring:** A hot shower pouring over a cliff decorates one side of a pool hidden 30 feet above the river. This one's big enough to pack maybe half

101

*The upper pool at Pine Flats Hot Spring features a steamy hot shower at one end.*

a dozen human sardines side by side and hot enough to turn them into lobsters. Cooler pools at the bottom collect the runoff from the showerbath above, and a large swimming hole at the river's edge adds the final touch. Those who prefer more privacy can wade along the base of the cliff to find yet another hot pool hidden in the rocks.

# 28 Kirkham Hot Springs

**General description:** Hot waterfalls and body-full bubblies on the South Fork Payette River below a highway campground, east of Lowman in Boise National Forest. Swimwear a must, at least before dark. Elevation 3,900 feet.

**Directions:** Drive four miles east of Lowman on State Route 21. Cross the bridge to Kirkham Campground and park at the west end. Follow a short path down to the river. The springs aren't marked on the forest map.

**The hot springs:** In plain view below the highway, these popular pools are frequently filled with boisterous teenagers and large family groups. The rock and sand pools, interspersed with steaming showers, come in all sizes, shapes, and temperatures. Kids of all ages love to leap off the rocks into deep holes in the river, and older folks can be seen scattered about on boulders dozing in the sun. The adjacent campground adds to the congestion here, and it's usually Winnebago City on summer weekends. Try early mornings or the winter months.

*Sun worshippers at Kirkham Hot Springs enjoy a simultaneous soak and hot shower.*

# HOT SPRING 27 *Pine Flats Hot Spring*
# HOT SPRINGS 28 *Kirkham Hot Springs*

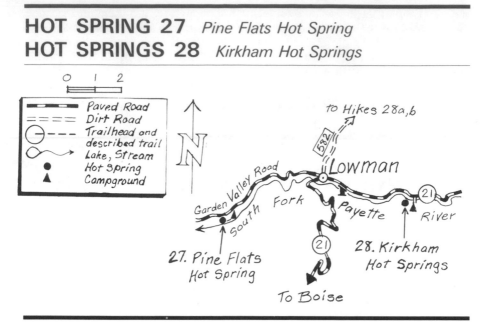

O  I  2

**Legend:**
- ▬▬▬ Paved Road
- ════ Dirt Road
- ⊝ - - - Trailhead and described trail
- ◡→ Lake, Stream
- ● Hot Spring
- ▲ Campground

N

to Hikes 28a, b

582

Lowman

Garden Valley Road

South Fork

Payette River

21

21

27. Pine Flats Hot Spring

28. Kirkham Hot Springs

To Boise

# HIKE 28a *Red Mountain Loop*

**General description:** A strenuous 10-mile, round-trip day climb (including a 4.5-mile, partially cross-country loop) to a viewpoint and off-trail lakes below, not far from Kirkham Hot Springs.
**Elevation gain and loss:** 2,560 feet (1,180 feet to start of loop; loop, 1,380 feet).
**Trailhead elevation:** 6,280 feet.
**High point:** Red Mountain Lookout, 8,722 feet.
**Maps:** Cache Creek and Miller Mtn. East 7.5-minute USGS quads; Boise National Forest.

**Finding the trailhead:** Take State Route 21 to Lowman and turn north on Forest Road 582. Drive 12 dusty miles toward Bear Valley, then turn right on Clear Creek Road (515) and go six bumpy miles to a roadblock with grassy space nearby for horses and a few cars. The new trailhead has been moved a mile back from the end of the road.

**The hike:** A brisk climb up a mountainside carpeted with wildflowers leads to a lookout crowning the rocky summit of Red Mountain. Look straight down on three lakes and out across a sea of green ridges and valleys to the Salmon River Mountains and the Sawtooths. The bird's-eye view is worth the climb, and a cross-country scramble down past the Red Mountain Lakes loops back to a connecting trail. With time to spare, you could continue from this point along a scenic ridge route ending at Bonneville Hot Springs in 20 miles (Hike 28b).

Walk the last road-mile to the register box and Clear Creek Trail. The route soon crosses Rough Creek and follows a second creekbed up a wooded slope,

*Three of Red Mountain's small lakes are visible to the east beneath the 8,722-foot summit.*

then veers away to climb through chaparral followed by open meadows. Turn left at a signed junction onto the lookout spur and switchback north toward the summit. In early summer, you'll pass patches of flaming Indian paintbrush, Red Mountain heath, and Mariposa lilies along the way. Take a break to enjoy the broad view from the lookout at 8,722 feet, four miles from the new trailhead.

To reach the nearest lake, just east of the summit, pick your route carefully down the precipitous slope past a small pond on your left. Circle the blue-green lake, rimmed by tall trees, on a faint path along the north shore and hop across its outlet. Next, scramble east down a wooded gulley to reach the largest of the Red Mountain Lakes at 7,850 feet. The deep green surface mirrors a wall of pines and firs.

Angle due south through a rocky cleft and pass a long pond on your right. Next, turn southeast to pass one more lake on your left (last chance to fill your canteen). Pick the easiest route south down a grassy slope to intersect Kirkham Ridge Trail two miles below the summit. Unless you plan to continue the 14 scenic miles from here to Bonneville (see below), turn right for .5 mile on Kirkham Ridge Trail (145) and right again on Clear Creek Trail. Follow it west past the lookout spur, then back out the way you came in.

# HIKE 28b *Red Mountain to Bonneville Hot Springs*

**General description:** A strenuous 20-mile, one-way overnighter linking the climb over Red Mountain with overviews of the Sawtooths en route to hot dips farther up the highway.
**Elevation gain and loss:** +4,480 feet, -6,080 feet.
**Trailhead elevation:** 6,280 feet.
**High point:** Red Mountain Lookout, 8,722 feet.

*The Link Trail offers many views of the Sawtooths on the hike from Red Mountain to Bonneville Hot Springs.*

**Maps:** Cache Creek, Miller Mtn. East, Bull Trout Point, and Eightmile Mtn. 7.5-minute USGS quads; Boise National Forest.

**Finding the trailhead:** Drive about 19 miles northeast of Lowman on State Route 21 and leave a car at Bonneville Campground. Shuttle a second car about 37 miles to the trailhead on Clear Creek Road. See Hike 28a for road access.

**The hike:** The Link Trail may well provide not only the most spectacular views of any hike in Boise Forest but also the best vantage point for seeing the entire length of the Sawtooth range. The route parallels the course of these jagged peaks from just enough distance for the hiker to absorb their full impact. For mile after mile along the sharp crest, the trail offers breathtaking views as it winds south toward State Route 21.

This hike combines the climb over Red Mountain with a trek along the Link Trail ending in a total of 20 miles at Bonneville Campground and Hot Springs. It's suggested as a one-way trip as the elevation gain is much more gradual in this direction. (There's a grueling gain of 2,920 feet in the first four miles when hiked from the lower end.) The only drawback is the car shuttle involved. See Hike 28a for the route over Red Mountain from Clear Creek Trailhead.

When you drop south from the Red Mountain lakes, you'll intersect Kirkham Ridge Trail (145) at six miles, 7,680 feet. Turn left for another two miles to reach the Link Trail. There's a campsite with a broad view but no water by the junction of Clear Creek and Kirkham Ridge Trails, at 7,600 feet, and a few more grassy spots in the area where Eightmile Creek crosses Kirkham Ridge Trail.

Turn south onto the upper end of the Link Trail (148) at eight miles, 7,480 feet. Climb the ridge above Eightmile Creek and enjoy the views over your shoulder of the many small lakes fanning out beneath the rugged east face of Red Mountain. The high point on the trail (8,120 feet) traverses the side of an unnamed peak. Soon, you'll reach a narrow saddle with the first view to the Sawtooths.

The next stretch crosses the shady side of another peak that may still have snow patches in late July. The path then drops 760 feet down a canyon to reach Castro Creek at 11 miles, 7,360 feet. Cross on logs to a large camping area in a clearing—the best on the Link Trail and the only year-around water source.

The trail continues south along Castro Creek and then climbs to a knoll with another vista. For the next few miles, it dips and rises along the crest at around 7,300 feet. Near a sign marked "East Fork", you'll pass a few camp-sites with access to early-season creek water.

This prime stretch offers magnificent panoramas as it slowly winds south to pass beneath the 7,871-foot summit of Eightmile Mountain at 15.5 miles. You'll get a close-up look up Grandjean Canyon (Hikes 30a,b) before plunging a nonstop 2,920 feet in four miles to the base of the mountain.

When you reach the register box at the lower end of the Link Trail, you'll be just .5 mile from your car. Cut left through the woods on a faint path that leads down a gulley and intersects the dirt road to reach Bonneville Campground and Hot Springs at 20 miles, 4,680 feet.

*"Rain-check":* *The first time I was here, it started spitting rain as I arrived at the Link Trail. By the time I reached the top, there was almost zero visibility.*

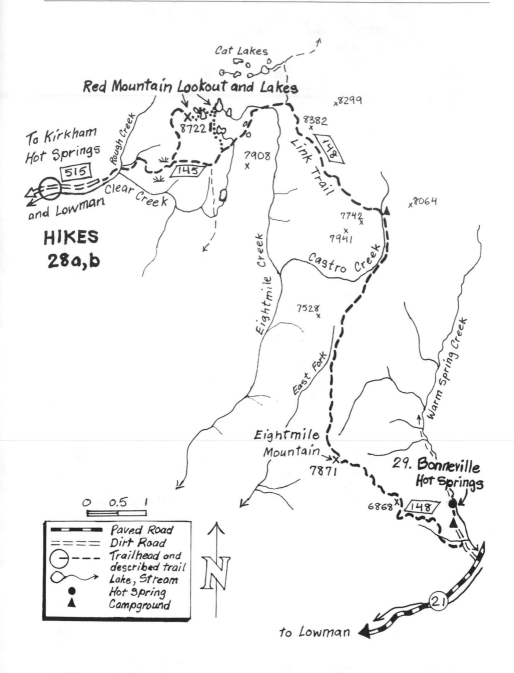

Cat Lakes

Red Mountain Lookout and Lakes

To Kirkham
Hot Springs

and Lowman

**HIKES
28a,b**

Rough Creek

Clear Creek

515

145

7908
x

8722
x

x8299

8382
x

148

Link Trail

x8064

7742
x

7941
x

Castro Creek

7528
x

Eightmile Creek

East Fork

Warm Spring Creek

Eightmile
Mountain

7871
x

29. Bonneville
Hot Springs

6868 x
148

to Lowman

21

0    0.5    1

Paved Road
Dirt Road
Trailhead and
described trail
Lake, Stream
Hot Spring
Campground

N

A cold wind seemed to be gusting from all directions at once, and the drizzle increased to a driving downpour. The trail turned into a creek that flowed past me as I sloshed up every hill. It reversed direction on the downhill stretches, and ponds formed on the level spaces between grades. I could barely make out my wet running shoes, much less the sweeping vistas I'd been anticipating.

When I reached the campsite on Castro Creek, I found to my horror that everything in my pack was soaked—even my sleeping bag! This left me no choice but to hike on out. I splashed uphill, downhill, across a pond only to repeat this dreary sequence mile after mile as the cold rain turned to sleet and hail. I reached the dry refuge of my car just after dark and the warm haven of Bonneville shortly thereafter—determined to try again for the gold next season!

# 29 Bonneville Hot Springs

**General description:** Private bathing and communal soaking in a wooded canyon near a family campground, northeast of Lowman in Boise National Forest. Keep swimwear within reach. Elevation 4,700 feet.

**Directions:** Follow State Route 21 about 19 miles northeast of Lowman to Bonneville Campground and park at the far end. Follow a creekside path .25 mile north to the springs. (See Hike 28b for a ridgeline trip ending up here.) The springs are marked on the forest map.

**The hot springs:** There is no time a hot soak is more welcome than right after a cold hike (see "Rain-check" above). The relief is immediate and the contrast unforgettable! Bonneville is a haven on such a day. A rustic bathhouse straddles the outflow, and hoses channel 103-degree water into a knee-deep wooden tub which can be drained and refilled after each use. Your clothes stay dry while your tired body gets wet. Sheer luxury!

The springs flow past the bathhouse and tumble directly over a rocky cliff into three new pools, with gradational temperatures, that span Warm Spring Creek. The largest is a clear, sandy-bottomed gem that measures a good 25 by 30 feet; users have built a masonry dam from boulders edged with a giant driftwood log. Steaming tendrils from other springs trickle down the bank into several smaller pools downstream.

Rumor has it that the Forest Service has no plans to rip out these lovely new pools as they periodically do with so many of the ones patched together with scuzzy sheets of plastic. If bathers continue to treat them with respect, it looks like these five-star soaks will be here to stay.

*These new creek-wide soakers at Bonneville are well engineered and a major improvement to an already great spot.*

# 30 Sacajawea Hot Springs

**General description:** Roadside hot dips on the South Fork Payette River, near the Grandjean trailhead into the Sawtooths, northeast of Lowman in Boise National Forest. Nudity a no-no before dark. Elevation 5,000 feet.

**Directions:** Drive about 21 miles northeast of Lowman on State Route 21 (two miles past Bonneville) and turn right on the graded forest road to Grandjean (524). Drive 4.6 miles to Waipiti Creek junction and continue .6 mile. Park wherever you can find space and climb down the rocks to the pools. Sacajawea isn't shown on the forest map.

**The hot springs:** A large number of soaker-friendly pools of all sizes and shapes line a beach along the scenic river. The outflow from many springs, at temperatures up to 108 degrees, cools as it fans out down the bank, and the pool temperatures can be fine-tuned by adding river water. Another welcome refuge for weary hikers, Sacajawea, is found just a mile from one of the principal gateways into the Sawtooths. You couldn't ask for a nicer finish to any hike.

# HIKE 30a  *Trail Creek Lakes*

**General description:** A strenuous 12-mile, round-trip day hike or overnighter climbing to timberline meadows and lakes in the Sawtooth Wilderness, near Sacajawea Hot Springs.
**Elevation gain and loss:** 3,085 feet.
**Trailhead elevation:** 5,160 feet.
**High point:** Upper Trail Creek Lake, 8,245 feet.
**Maps:** Grandjean and Stanley Lake 7.5-minute USGS quads; Sawtooth National Forest.

**Finding the trailhead:** Follow the directions above to Sacajawea Hot Springs and continue another mile southeast to the end of the road. The trailhead for both Trail Creek and Baron Lakes is at the east end of Grandjean Campground.

**The hike:** Each of these small glacial lakes has a character all its own. As the route rises closer to timberline, rocky knolls and basins of pink Sawtooth granite gradually replace tree-studded lower slopes, and tight clusters of subalpine fir reluctantly give way to a land of stark rock.

Walk east through woods for the first .25 mile and bridge Trail Creek to a junction. The right fork heads south to Baron Lakes (Hike 30b), and the left fork (453) climbs Trail Creek. You'll have to cross five times on logs or rocks on the way up the narrow V-shaped canyon. This could be dangerous during high water. The route enters the wilderness just before the fourth ford, then snakes up a steep slope to the Trail Creek junction with a 2,400-foot gain in four miles.

Turn right on Trail 483, cross the creek one last time in a boggy patch, then climb a ridge to a viewpoint looking down the precipitous canyon. The final piece of eroded track zigzags over a rocky bench, passes some creekside campsites in a grove of tall trees, then tops a last short pitch to come to rest by the first of the lakes at 4.75 miles, 8,000 feet.

Lower Trail Creek Lake has a waterfall at its far end. Level campsites at the outlet look out across the blue-green water to granite walls rimming the thickly wooded basin. A conical peak juts up from the southeast shore, and brook trout ripple the surface late in the day. Circle the northern shore on a fisherman's path to a flat with a few more campsites in the woods.

The path climbs a slope just beyond the clearing to reach the second lake at 8,225 feet. The wide basin here has fewer tall trees, and small meadows are interspersed with outcrops of rock. Mount Regan stands out at 10,190 feet a mile to the east. Follow the north shore and, as you near the end, pick a

*The riverside pools at Sacajawea Hot Springs take on a new look every summer.*

cross-country route heading north. Scramble up a talus slope and work your way through a maze of granite knolls and small ponds to reach the third lake at six miles, 8,245 feet.

A moonscape of boulders and granite slabs rims the shoreline of Upper Trail Creek Lake, and tiny wildflowers dot the subalpine meadows. A scree slope tails out across the shallow center of the lake; from the last stone you can see every detail on the rocky bottom.

*"Slip-sliding away": When I reached the uppermost lake, I slithered down the talus to fill my canteen at the deep end. Just as I leaned forward with bottle in hand, all the rocks around me suddenly started to move. Before I had time to react, the rocks and I were sliding together into the lake! I didn't really object to the unexpected swim, although I would rather have had time to leave my clothes, boots, and lunchbag behind. The thought foremost in my mind as the cold water engulfed me was of my poor camera. This trusty old Olympus, which had survived untold watery adventures in our travels together, had finally met its Waterloo.*

---

# HIKE 30b  *Baron Lakes*

**General description:** A moderate 21.5-mile, round-trip overnighter featuring alpine lakes and panoramic views in the Sawtooth Wilderness, near Sacajawea Hot Springs.
**Elevation gain and loss:** +3,440 feet, -100 feet.
**Trailhead elevation:** 5,160 feet.
**High point:** Upper Baron Lake, 8,505 feet.
**Maps:** Grandjean, Stanley Lake, and Warbonnet Peak 7.5-minute USGS quads; Sawtooth National Forest.

**Finding the trailhead:** Follow the road access for Hike 30a.

**The hike:** The name "Sawtooths" conjures up images of sharp craggy peaks rising above serrated ridges. The Baron Lakes country is the Sawtooths at their best. The two deep-blue upper lakes lie in glacial bowls hemmed in by peach and rose-hued walls of Sawtooth granite. Stands of fir thin out as you climb from one lake to the next, with colorful rock becomimg ever more dominant. The view back across the lakes from Baron Divide takes in countless rocky spires and peaks.

This is the quieter of two equally scenic routes to the popular Baron Lakes. It travels up the U-shaped glacial canyon of Baron Creek to reach Upper Baron Lake in 10.75 miles. The east-side trailhead at Redfish Lake is three miles shorter. You could see the best of both routes by entering at Grandjean, crossing over Baron Divide, and exiting at Redfish Lake in 18.5 miles (see Hike 38c).

Stroll east for the first .25 mile to a junction. The left fork climbs to Trail Creek Lakes (Hike 30a), and the right turns south to Baron Lakes. Follow the level South Fork Payette River (Trail 452) 1.5 miles southeast, then turn east onto Baron Creek Trail (101) and climb two miles along the grassy slope above the wide canyon. Just beyond a creek ford, North Baron Trail branches off to the left, climbing to Sawtooth Lake in six miles (see Hike 38a). The main

# HOT SPRINGS 30  *Sacajawea Hot Springs*
# HIKE 30a  *Trail Creek Lakes*
# HIKE 30b  *Baron Lakes*

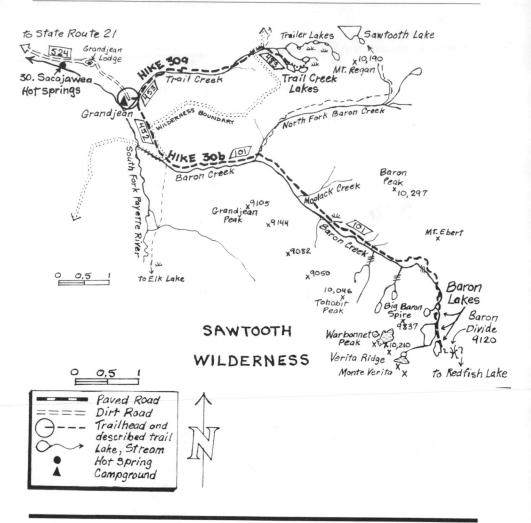

canyon veers southeast for several miles as the rocky walls slowly converge.

Ford Moolack Creek at five miles, 6,200 feet. This major stream, set in a grove of cottonwoods, is followed by several tiny creeks lined with wildflowers and quaking aspen. The grassy slopes between fords are brushed with stands of spruce and fir. As the walls finally close in, you'll have a good view of Tohobit Falls and Peak on the opposite bank at seven miles. Next in line are Warbonnet Falls and Peak. The trail then hairpins 800 feet up the headwall alongside the roaring Baron Creek Falls. Above, the trail crosses the first bridge after the one at Trail Creek nine miles back.

Little Baron Lake lies in a shallow basin off the trail a short hop west of the third stream crossing. It has several uncrowded campsites in the trees near the outlet. Subalpine firs ring the small lake and give it acres of privacy but limited views.

Baron Lake is the next stop, at 10.25 miles, 8,312 feet. A jagged wall of granite across the lake is mirrored in the sapphire-blue water. The most level camp-

*Upper Baron Lake reflects a clear image of 9,837-foot Big Baron Spire.*

sites lie on each side of the outlet facing the view. If these are full, try the west shore across from the trail.

The two lower lakes are bordered to the west by 9,837-foot Big Baron Spire. Just south of this flat faced peak, the sawtoothed silhouette of Verita Ridge parallels Baron Lake to the west and eclipses 10,210-foot Warbonnet Peak. Southwest of the halfmile-long lake rise the two towering crests of Monte Verita.

The short trail to Upper Baron climbs the ridge that separates them, and the only semi-level campsite is right beside the path where you first drop into the rocky basin at 10.75 miles, 8,505 feet. The continuing trail over the divide climbs sharply above the east shore, with a broader view at every switchback, and Baron Lake becomes more visible just below the upper lake. From Baron Divide, at a skyscraping 9,120 feet, the Sawtooths seem to stretch out forever!

---

# 31 Bear Valley Hot Springs

## HIKE 31a  To Bear Valley Hot Springs

**General description:** An almost easy 7-mile, round-trip day hike or overnighter to a chain of pearls locked up in the River of No Return Wilderness, northeast of Lowman. Swimwear superfluous baggage.
**Elevation gain and loss:** +160 feet, -320 feet.
**High point:** Trailhead, 6,360 feet.
**Low point:** Hot springs, 6,200 feet.
**Maps:** River of No Return Wilderness, South half (Forest Service contour map) or Blue Bunch Mtn. and Cape Horn Lakes 7.5-minute USGS quads; Boise National Forest.

**Finding the trailhead:** On State Route 21, drive about 37 miles northeast of Lowman or 21 miles northwest of Stanley. Turn west on Forest Road 82/579 signed to Bruce Meadows and Boundary Creek. At about eight miles, a small sign marks the turnoff to Marsh Creek Trail and Fir Creek Campground (if you pass the airstrip you've gone too far). Park at Fir Creek Pack Bridge, the trailhead for both Bear Valley Hot Springs and Blue Bunch Mountain. The springs are marked only on the USGS map.

**The hike:** Imagine a string of clear pools of perfect soaking temperature drawing you from one to the next down to the edge of a lively creek. The uppermost and largest is sheltered under a canopy of evergreenery, while the creekside dips, lined with sun warmed rocks, give a feeling of openness and contact with the stream. The setting is as close to perfection as nature allows.

Bear Valley Creek has a claim to fame apart from its hot springs. It joins Marsh Creek just downstream to become the headwaters of the Middle Fork Salmon River—one of the star attractions in the River of No Return Wilderness (see Hikes 32/33a and 45/46a). The trail was used heavily at one time by salmon fishermen but has seen little use in the last ten years due to a closure designed to protect the spawning salmon. Chances are good that you'll have the hot pools to yourself.

*This creekside dip is the last link in the chain at Bear Valley Hot Springs.*

Turn right across the bridge onto Marsh Creek Trail (12). Follow the creek east for the first easy 1.5 miles, then watch for a spot in a large meadow (marked with orange survey ribbons tied to bushes on each side) where the trail crosses it and disappears into the woods. This ford would be suicidal during high water; the fast moving stream is a good 20 yards wide and often knee-deep through mid-August. Next, the path winds through an intricate tangle of lodgepole pines strewn about on the ground like an oversized child's game of pick-up sticks.

Watch closely for a tree on your left in 3.5 miles that bears the hand carved message "HS". Take your choice of faint paths winding down a geothermal slope. Don't be discouraged when you reach the bottom and find only one murky, ankle deep pool filled with algae. Stroll downstream to a larger flow and track it past a grassy campsite to a chain of five-star gems dropping step by step to the creek's edge.

It should be mentioned in passing that there's an alternate route that saves fording the creek as well as .5 mile of walking. It's a primitive path that follows the south bank from Fir Creek Campground to the point where the Forest Service trail crosses over. The catch is that it erodes away to almost nothing traversing a slippery stretch well up the steep bank. It's not a route for small children or anyone afraid of heights. The prudent choice would be to hold off until late August and take the official trail.

# HIKE 31b  *Blue Bunch Mountain*

**General description:** A moderate 10-mile, round-trip day climb to a mountaintop in the River of No Return Wilderness, near Bear Valley Hot Springs.
**Elevation gain and loss:** +2,480 feet, -100 feet.
**Trailhead elevation:** 6,360 feet.
**High point:** Blue Bunch Mountain, 8,743 feet.
**Maps:** Same as Hike 31a minus the Cape Horn Lakes USGS quad.

**Finding the trailhead:** Follow the road access for Hike 31a.

**The hike:** The serious hiker with a day to spare and energy to burn after the trip to Bear Valley Hot Springs might consider a second outing from the same trailhead. This brisk climb has a gain of 2,480 feet in five miles but tops off with views of Red Mountain to the southwest (see Hikes 28a,b) and Cape Horn Mountain to the southeast.

Turn left across the bridge onto Blue Bunch Mountain Trail (13). The path crosses the wilderness boundary and climbs north through thickly wooded slopes scarred by a recent fire to reach Blue Bunch Ridge in about four miles. Beyond a sheepherder's cabin and spring, the route becomes hard to trace in spots. Continue north along the tapering ridge for the final two miles and enjoy increasing glimpses of the valleys spread out below. The trail finally peters out, along with the weary hiker, at the viewpoint on the summit.

# HIKE 31a *To Bear Valley Hot Springs*
# HIKE 31b *Blue Bunch Mountain*

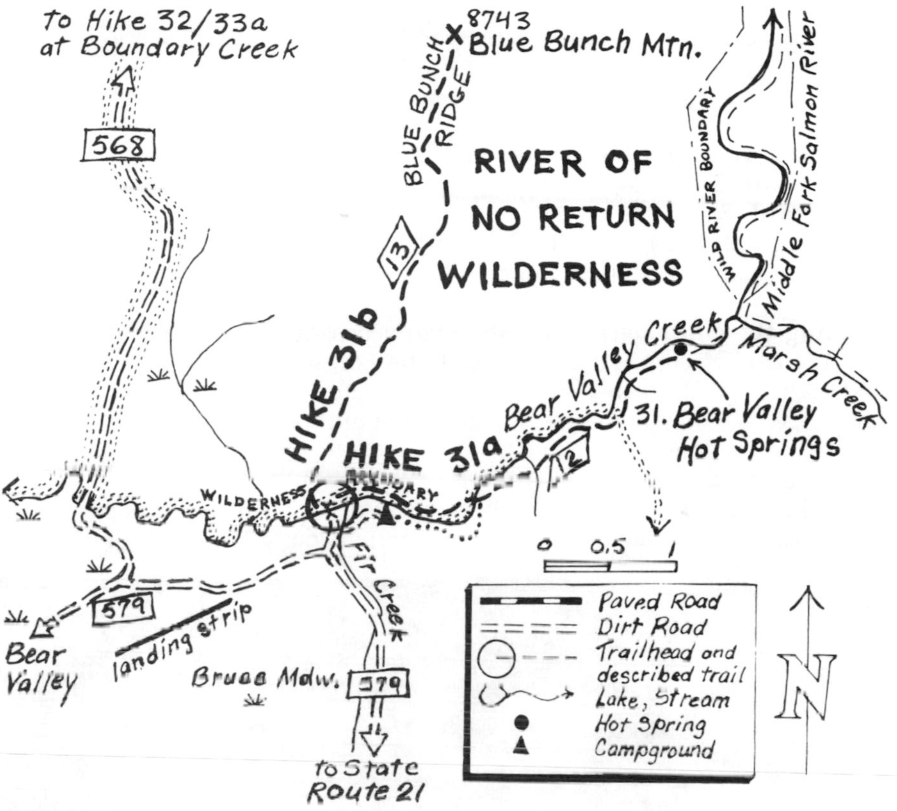

To Hike 32/33a
at Boundary Creek

568

8743
× Blue Bunch Mtn.

BLUE BUNCH RIDGE

WILD RIVER BOUNDARY

Middle Fork Salmon River

RIVER OF
NO RETURN
WILDERNESS

13

HIKE 31b

Bear Valley Creek

Marsh Creek

HIKE 31a

31. Bear Valley
Hot Springs

12

WILDERNESS BOUNDARY

579

Fir Creek

Bear
Valley

landing strip

Bruce Mdw. 579

to State
Route 21

0    0.5    1

Paved Road
Dirt Road
Trailhead and
described trail
Lake, Stream
Hot Spring
Campground

N

## HIKE 32/33a  *To Trail Flat & Sheepeater Hot Springs*

**General description:** A moderate 26-mile, round-trip backpack to a double bubble known only to river rats, in the Middle Fork Salmon River Canyon of the River of No Return Wilderness, northeast of Lowman. "Naked bodies welcome" is the tradition.

**Elevation gain and loss:** +500 feet, -1,100 feet.

**High point:** Trailhead, 5,800 feet.

**Low point:** Sheepeater, 5,200 feet.

**Best map:** Middle Fork of the Salmon (detailed Forest Service contour map and river guide); Challis National Forest.

**Finding the trailhead:** Follow the road access for Hike 31a, but continue past the landing strip. Turn right (north) on Forest Road 568 and drive to the end of the road (23 dusty miles from State Route 21). Be sure to check in with the ranger at Boundary Creek Launch Area and Trailhead. Both springs are shown on the map.

**The hike:** Two remote hot springs lie six miles apart near the upper end of the Middle Fork Salmon River. The streamside soaks at Trail Flat are

*Late summer is the perfect time for backpackers to visit Trail Flat Hot Springs.*

submerged at high water but should be fine by midsummer, while Sheepeater Camp's secluded dips lie on a rocky terrace well above the river's grasp. The 100-mile long river (the only navigable stream of such length in the northwest where powerboats are banned) lies within the National Wild and Scenic Rivers System of the River of No Return Wilderness.

The route to both bubblies follows the west side of the river downstream from Boundary Creek, a launch site where rafts splash down over a 100-foot high ramp. By around mid-August, the rafts are flown to a lower put-in at Pistol Creek. From this time on, the hot pools and nearby campsites should be nearly deserted, the side creeks safe to ford, and the trail high and dry above the river. The access road is open until mid-October.

The Middle Fork Trail (1) follows a jeep road for the first mile or so over wooded hills, passing a private airstrip and side trails at Sulphur and Prospect Creeks; it reaches the river at four miles near a point overlooking a turquoise pool, by the bridge over Ramshorn Creek.

The path briefly hugs the river, then climbs well up the bank. Traversing this slope, it seems to drape loosely from the base of one anchoring tree to the next like a Christmas tree chain drooping from bough to bough. There are no views until you reach an open hill above Trail Flat. Once you spot the gravel bar, you can usually make out the steam rising from the pools. Drop down a rocky slope to reach the campground at seven miles, 5,400 feet.

Trail Flat has one large, very hot pool midway along the beach and increasingly cooler ones fanning out to the river's edge. There's an open bench with convenient campsites directly above the soaking pools. Check out the 2-sided outhouse hiding behind a tree just off the trail—the odd shape seems to be

*The Middle Fork Trail between Trail Flat and Sheepeater Hot Springs offers many views up and down the rugged canyon.*

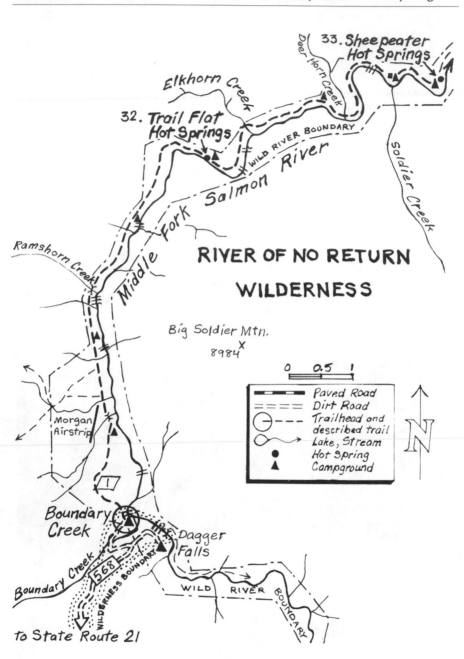

33. Sheepeater Hot Springs

Elkhorn Creek

Deer Horn Creek

32. Trail Flat Hot Springs

WILD RIVER BOUNDARY

Middle Fork Salmon River

Soldier Creek

Ramshorn Creek

**RIVER OF NO RETURN**

**WILDERNESS**

Big Soldier Mtn.
8984 X

0   0.5   1

Paved Road
Dirt Road
Trailhead and
described trail
Lake, Stream
Hot Spring
Campground

N

Morgan Airstrip

Boundary Creek

Dagger Falls

568

WILDERNESS BOUNDARY

Boundary Creek

WILD RIVER BOUNDARY

to State Route 21

quite the fashion in campsites along the Middle Fork.

The 12-mile round trip from Trail Flat to Sheepeater is the most scenic stretch of the hike; it can be done in one long day with ample time to enjoy the soaking pools at both ends. The route stays close to the river much of the way, and when it climbs it keeps it in sight. Hills wooded with tall ponderosas alternate with boulder-strewn slopes, and there are many pleasant views up and down the canyon.

About a mile below Trail Flat, the path drops down to ford Elkhorn Creek, which may be impassable at high water. It climbs and then dips again to cross Deer Horn Creek on an upstream log at 10 miles. When you pass Joe Bump's log cabin, followed by a rustic grave marked Elmer "Set Trigger" Purcell, prospector/trapper, 1936, you'll be in the home stretch.

Watch for a square soaking pool lined with split logs in a clearing off to the left at 13 miles. Big enough to house a small army, the semi-landlocked pool makes a cozy (though a bit cloudy) cocoon. Shortly beyond it are three tiny pools tucked up against the bank. These hotter dips have an ample flow to keep them clean but no handy means of lowering the temperature. You can track the broad outflow down to two slightly cooler soaks hidden in the woods. There's a large camping area by the river and another in a clearing just above.

# E. AROUND ATLANTA

The Atlanta trailhead into the western Sawtooths is located 45 paved plus 45 very dusty miles northeast of Boise. It's the longest approach both for driving and for hiking but also by far the least crowded. Trailhead soaks add much to the appeal as does the tiny backwoods town. From Atlanta and Chattanooga Hot Springs, wilderness buffs can follow the Boise River up to alpine lakes and panoramic views (Hikes 35a-c).

**Getting to Atlanta:** On State Route 21, drive 19 miles northeast of Idaho City (or 15 miles south of Lowman) to Edna Creek Campground. The next 30 miles of dirt are graded and signed "to Atlanta". The route forms two big scallops on the forest map: the first (Forest Road 384) covers the 12-mile stretch to the North Fork Boise River; the second road (327) covers the 18 miles to the Middle Fork. Only the final 15-mile grind up the Middle Fork Road (268) is painfully rocky and slow.

# 34 Atlanta Hot Springs

**General description:** A roadside hot dip near the Atlanta trailhead into the Sawtooths, east of Idaho City in Boise National Forest. Keep a swimsuit handy. Elevation 5,500 feet.

**Directions:** Follow the directions above to Atlanta. Continue a mile north-

123

east on the road to Power Plant Recreation Area, then watch for a large pond on your right. A spur just beyond it has room for a car or two to park, and a short path leads to the pool. The springs aren't marked on the forest map.

**The hot springs:** A small but comfortable soaker with a split-log bench sits in a grassy clearing in the woods a scant .5 mile from the Atlanta trailhead. Spring water is diverted into the rock and sand pool by a length of hose, and the temperature hovers around 100 degrees. The runoff flows into the pond—which doubles as a fine swimming hole. The setting is marred only by the nearby road.

*"Over and out":* As I climbed out of this pool one day, I suddenly remembered a phone call that I'd promised a friend. I sped into town only to find that the only contact with the outside world in these parts was a radiotelephone on the counter of the cafe. I was briefed by the short-order cook on the art of conducting a one-way conversation. Precision timing is required. You push a button to transmit and release to receive. Release too soon and your sentence is cut off; release too late and you lose the reply. Remember to end every remark with a loud "OVER", or the other party won't know it's time to speak. As I stood there fumbling with the button and shouting birthday greetings into the microphone, I must have provided the townfolk of Atlanta with the best live entertainment they'd had in some time!

*This bird's-eye view of Chattanooga Hot Springs is from the trailhead parking area on the cliff above.*

124

# 35 Chattanooga Hot Springs

**General description:** A five star soaker on the Middle Fork Boise River near the Atlanta trailhead into the Sawtooths, east of Idaho City in Boise National Forest. Swimwear optional. Elevation 5,460 feet.

**Directions:** Follow the directions above to Atlanta and continue a mile northeast on the road to Power Plant Recreation Area. Just west of the pond by Atlanta Hot Springs, look for a left turn marked by a tree that bisects the road. Follow a short spur north to an unofficial camping area. Park here and choose between two steep paths dropping down to the pool. Chattanooga isn't shown on the forest map.

**The hot springs:** Bubbly springs cascade over a cliff into a large, knee-deep pool lined with rocks. The clear pool has a sandy bottom, and the temperature seems to stay a steady perfect. This topnotch retreat, just .5 mile from the trailhead for the following hikes, is tucked between the base of the 100-foot cliff and the nearby river. The jagged Sawtooths across the canyon form a dramatic backdrop to the setting. This is a great place to pause and unwind between the rigors of a long, dusty trail and those of an even longer, bumpy road!

# HIKE 35a *Spangle Lakes*

**General description:** A rugged 31-mile, round-trip backpack featuring alpine meadows and lakes in the heart of the Sawtooth Wilderness, near Atlanta and Chattanooga Hot Springs.
**Elevation gain and loss:** +3,480 feet, -320 feet.
**Trailhead elevation:** 5,440 feet.
**High point:** Upper Spangle Lake, 8,600 feet.
**Maps:** Atlanta East and Mt. Everly 7.5 minute USGS quads; Sawtooth National Forest.

**Finding the trailhead:** Follow the directions above to Atlanta and continue 1.5 miles northeast to Power Plant Recreation Area (.5 mile past both hot springs). The trail sign is located on the right side of a large meadow at the campground entrance. Give the car a well earned rest and put your boots to work.

**The hike:** A bonsai effect of delicate meadows, rock gardens, and dwarfed, twisted trees is the setting for Little Spangle Lake. Upper Spangle is a deep blue circle rimmed by thick woods and cream colored granite walls. The basin sits on the threshold of the magnificent high country, and lonesome campsites tempt the visitor to linger and explore farther (Hikes 35b,c). The price of admission is a lengthy access on a trail that doesn't give much to write home about for the first 12 miles—a gradual ascent through a uniform forest of Douglas-fir relieved by occasional meadows.

*Increasing glimpses of granite peaks and ridges above the river canyon ease the strain of the long climb to Spangle Lakes.*

The first few miles east on the Middle Fork Boise River Trail (460) are an easy stroll. The route then hairpins up a hill, and Leggit Lake Trail forks south from the top of a rocky knoll at 6,050 feet. Keep trudging northeast up the wooded canyon well above the river. Pass Mattingly Creek Trail junction in five miles and cross the creek itself in another .5 mile. This stream is a good late-season water source and has fine campsites on both sides of the log crossing.

The 4-mile stretch north to Rock Creek is a moderate climb up the east side of the canyon. A few campsites hide in the woods west of the trail at the end of a meadow .25 mile before the first river crossing. The route crosses two wide channels here in a rocky outwash that could be dangerous too early in the summer. Just beyond the second ford, at 6,400 feet, the trail splits. The left branch climbs Rock Creek to Timpa Lake, and the main trail turns east.

The trail crosses the river four times in the 3.5 miles to Flytrip Creek. Scout for footlogs hidden up or downstream. Next, wade a meadow with chin-high wildflowers and a view of Mattingly Peak over your shoulder. Later, the path reaches a few campsites in a flat where the river (just a small stream by now) splits into several channels and the trail disappears. Wade the stream and aim for a grove of tall trees ahead, where you'll find more campsites. The Flytrip Creek Trail junction (at 7,500 feet) branches off to your right.

A scenic side trip can be made up the steep 1.5-mile trail to Camp Lake at 8,500 feet. Follow a faint path southeast from its inlet to reach Heart Lake in another .25 mile. Low ridges separate the many tiny lakes just south and east. Beyond them rises the jagged crest of the Sawtooths topped by 10,651-foot Snowyside Peak. To explore these lakes, you'll need the Snowyside Peak 7.5-minute USGS quad.

The final 3-mile stretch offers broad views as the trail switchbacks up the headwall. Continue over the crest past a meadow to Little Spangle Lake. Peninsulas and inlets around the shallow basin offer a variety of photogenic scenes and a fresh outlook from every arm stretching across the pale blue water; rocky islands breaking the surface adopt a new shape from each viewpoint. An idyllic campsite lies across a small meadow at the northeast corner.

Cross a low ridge 200 yards north to reach Upper Spangle Lake at 8,600 feet. The large, circular lake is hemmed in by a steep basin crowded with subalpine fir, lodgepole and whitebark pine. The only decent campsites lie up a small valley on the northeast side. The Middle Fork Trail ends at Spangle Junction near the south shore. Two new trails begin here—both easy day trips from Spangle Lakes.

---

# HIKE 35b  *Spangle Lakes to Tenlake Basin & Ardeth Lake*

**General description:** A moderate 5-mile, round-trip day hike or overnighter from Spangle Lakes to more high views and lakes in the Sawtooth Wilderness.
**Elevation gain and loss:** +352 feet, -712 feet.
**Trailhead elevation:** 8,600 feet at Upper Spangle Lake.
**High point:** Spangle Summit, 8,952 feet.
**Maps:** Same as Hike 35a plus Mt. Everly 7.5-minute USGS quad.

# HIKE 35a  *Spangle Lakes*
# HIKE 35b  *Spangle Lake to Tenlake Basin & Ardeth Lake*
# HIKE 36c  *Spangle Lakes to Ingeborg, Rock Slide, & Benedict Lakes*

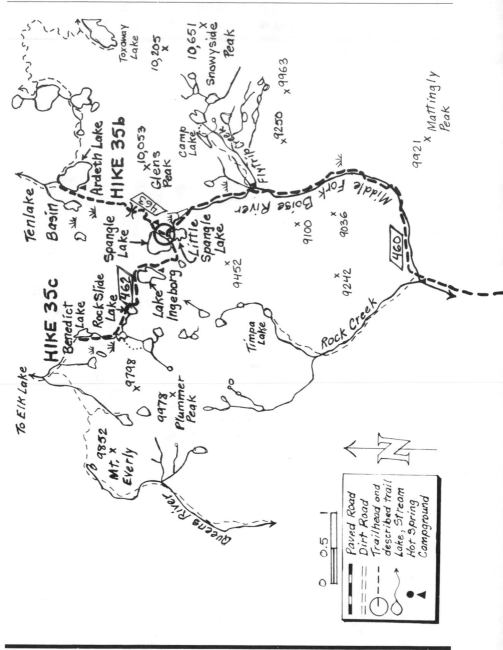

# HOT SPRINGS 34 *Atlanta Hot Springs*
# HOT SPRINGS 35 *Chattanooga Hot Springs*

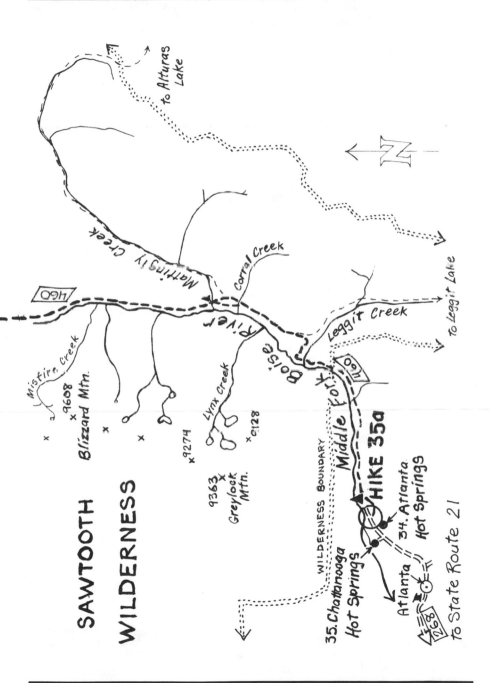

129

**Finding the trailhead:** Follow Hike 35a to Spangle Lakes.

**The hike:** Look south from Spangle Summit to jagged peaks rising above the river canyon far below. To the west, above Spangle Lake Basin, is the snow-capped escarpment by Lake Ingeborg. Look straight up at 10,053-foot Glens Peak to the east. To the north lies the rocky Tenlake Basin—you can count at least six of the many small lakes from here.

To get there, turn right (northeast) at Spangle Junction and climb the ridge above the east side of the lake on a well maintained trail (463). Enjoy the panoramic views from the 8,952-foot summit (the high point on the hike) just a mile up the trail.

Drop down the steep talus slope on the north side of the ridge. You may still find snow patches here in midsummer. The route passes just west of a marshy pond and continues north through a forest of subalpine fir and lodgepoles leading down to Ardeth Lake at 2.5 miles, 8,240 feet.

The path emerges from the woods to overlook beach campsites on the southwest shore. Follow the trail down the west side of the lake to more campsites and viewpoints near the outlet on the northwest side. There's a marvelous outlook from here of the permanent snowfields and jagged silhouette of Glens Peak mirrored in the clear water.

---

# HIKE 35c  *Spangle Lakes to Ingeborg, Rock Slide, & Benedict Lakes*

**General description:** A moderate 6-mile, round-trip day hike or overnighter from Spangle Lakes to the highest lake reached by trail in the Sawtooth Wilderness.
**Elevation gain and loss:** +320 feet, -640 feet.
**Trailhead elevation:** 8,600 feet at Upper Spangle Lake.
**High point:** 8,920 feet.
**Maps:** Same as Hike 35b.

**Finding the trailhead:** Follow Hike 35a to Spangle Lakes.

**The hike:** No trek to Spangle Lakes is complete without a side trip to these beautiful lakes. The lightly traveled route offers unlimited opportunities to explore and enjoy the magnificent alpine scenery on all sides. Don't miss it!

The trail (462) begins at Spangle Junction and zigzags up the steep basin on the southwest side. The grade tapers off near a small gem of a lake rimmed with granite walls. Bear northwest a mile across the 8,920-foot plateau to reach sky-high Lake Ingeborg at 8,890 feet (the highest major lake accessible by trail in the Sawtooths) on a bench between the Boise River and Benedict Creek drainages. Rosy granite juts above the western side; the shoreline is dotted with limber pine and subalpine fir between tiny campsites.

Circle the east side, then drop 200 feet to Rock Slide (a smaller lake in a similar setting) in another .75 mile. The trail descends through the maze of boulders that give the lake its present name. The label shown on the forest map, Robert Jackson Lake, came from a man who decided to name it after himself! When the USGS learned that Mr. Jackson was not only still alive but

*Rock Slide Lake earned its new name from the slide falling directly into the small triangular lake from a nearby peak.*

had no historical connection with the lake, they changed it to the present name.

The path follows the east side of Rock Slide Lake and descends a wooded hillside to a large pond. The meadow on the east shore is cut by serpentine channels that resemble dragons in an oriental rug pattern. Continue north across a marsh sprinkled with tiny wildflowers, then drop down a wooded ridge to reach Benedict Lake at three miles, 8,260 feet. Green meadows and a thick border of subalpine fir line the west wall, and two sharp peaks mark the south end of the valley.

# 36 Granite Creek Hot Spring

**General description:** A remote roadside hot dip on the Middle Fork Boise River, west of Atlanta in Boise National Forest. Swimsuits strongly advised. Elevation 5,400 feet.

**Directions:** Drive 15 very rocky miles west of Atlanta along the Middle Fork (Forest Road 268) past the junction of Forest Roads 156 south and 327 north. Continue 3.4 miles west (past Dutch Creek Guard Station) to a small pullout .5 mile east of a sign labeling Granite Creek. Park here and hop down the rocks to the pool. The spring isn't marked on the forest map.

**The hot spring:** Boulders line a riverside soaking pool right below a major logging road. The outflow from the nearby spring keeps the sandy-bottomed pool fairly clean, and the temperature can be lowered by removing a rock or two from the side by the river. This may be the best of several dips found at intervals farther downstream. Its only drawback is the proximity of the very dusty road.

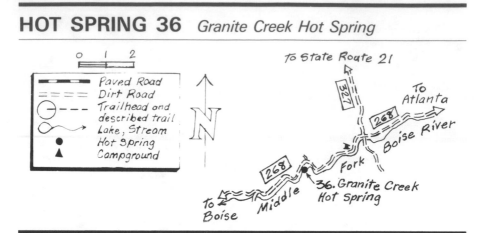

Paved Road
Dirt Road
Trailhead and described trail
Lake, Stream
Hot Spring
Campground

To State Route 21
To Atlanta
Boise River
36. Granite Creek Hot Spring
Fork
268
Middle
To Boise

# F. OUT OF KETCHUM & STANLEY

State Route 75 runs northwest of Ketchum through the Sawtooth National Recreation Area (SNRA); the eye-catching drive parallels the Salmon River and the jagged Sawtooth range. A number of roadside hot dips (37-41) in this area combine well with trips into the Smoky Mountains (Hikes 37a,b) and the eastern Sawtooths around Stanley (Hikes 38a-c). Next, a remote trail north of Sunbeam leads to five hot springs on Loon Creek in the River of No Return Wilderness (Hike 42a). Farther east, we find Slate Creek Hot Spring and a nearby path into the White Clouds (Hike 43a).

# 37 Russian John Hot Spring

**General description:** A roadside warm soak northwest of Ketchum in the SNRA. Skinnydippable. Elevation 6,900 feet.

**Directions:** From Ketchum, drive about 18 miles northwest on State Route 75. The turnoff is located 2.5 miles past Baker Creek Road (see Hikes 37a,b). Turn west onto a dirt road near milepost 146, then south to the parking area by the pool. The spring isn't marked on the forest map.

**The hot spring:** A huge pile of logs shelters an old sheepherder's soaking pool from sight of the busy highway 200 yards away. The clay bottom stirs up easily, and the temperature hovers around 85 degrees—on the lower edge of warm. The popularity of the small pool is probably due to its semi-secluded setting and to the fact that it's a long drive to the next dip.

# HOT SPRING 37   *Russian John Hot Spring*

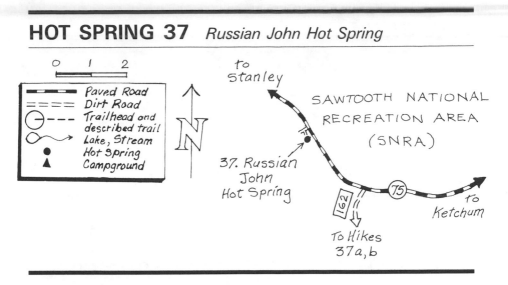

# HIKE 37a   *Baker Lake*

**General description:** A brisk 2-mile, round-trip stroll to a popular lake in the Smoky Mountains, near Russian John Hot Spring.
**Elevation gain and loss:** 880 feet.
**Trailhead elevation:** 7,920 feet.
**High point:** Baker Lake, 8,800 feet.
**Maps:** Baker Peak 7.5-minute USGS quad; Sawtooth National Forest.

**Finding the trailhead:** Follow the directions above to Baker Creek Road (Forest Road 162). Turn left and drive eight dusty miles to the road-end parking area and trail sign.

**The hike:** This pretty lake, a pleasant family outing, is well worth the short walk. Tall stands of fir rim the grassy shore, and pink granite cliffs cast their reflections in the clear water. Baker Lake Trail (138) starts off by crossing a branch of Baker Creek and then follows an old jeep track up a grassy hillside. Continue west on a sneaker-worn path that follows a wooded ridge leading up to the lake.

# HIKE 37a  *Baker Lake*

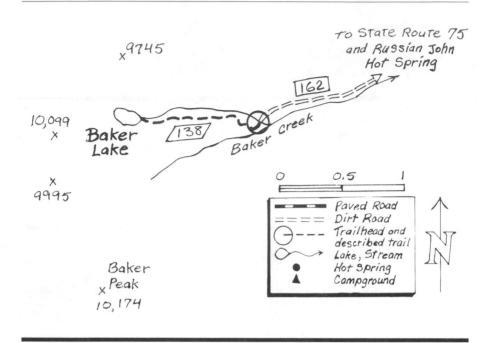

# HIKE 37b  *Norton Lakes Loop*

**General description:** A strenuous 5.5-mile, round-trip day hike (including a 3.5-mile, partially cross-country loop) to secluded lakes in the Smoky Mountains, near Russian John Hot Spring.
**Elevation gain and loss:** 1,840 feet (520 feet to start of loop; loop, 1,180 feet; to Upper Norton Lake, 140 feet).
**Trailhead elevation:** 7,640 feet.
**High point:** 9,300 feet.
**Maps:** Same as Hike 37a.

**Finding the trailhead:** Follow the road access above, taking Baker Creek Road six miles southwest to Norton Creek. Turn right on Norton Lake Road (170) and drive a bumpy mile to the end. Park wherever you can find room and dig out your boots.

**The hike:** Most visitors take the steep trail to the Norton Lakes, pause for lunch, and head back the way they came in. The adventurous hiker can make a loop that circles from Lower Norton Lake through a maze of granite ridges and basins past Big Lost and Smoky Lakes before dropping down a canyon to rejoin the trail. In addition to excellent scenery, the off-trail route offers the fun of exploration and discovery.

Wade the deep gulley of Norton Creek (this could be treacherous during high water). Turn right at the register box and climb the wooded west bank on Norton Lake Trail (135). Cross a side creek and continue up a valley with a view of a serrated ridge. The 2-mile trail to the lakes has a gain of 1,300 feet.

Lower Norton Lake is fringed with wildflowers spaced between stands of tall trees; rocky slopes back the far shore. Upper Norton is reached by a short path that climbs the flower-choked inlet.

Leave the trail behind at Lower Norton Lake and walk around either side to the west end. Pick a route heading due south up a scree-filled gulley. Cross over the lowest point on the ridge (and the highest point on the hike) at 9,300 feet. Bear right (southwest) as you descend the far side and head across a rocky valley leading to the next lake.

The moonscape setting for Big Lost Lake is a wide shoreline strewn with giant boulders; a jagged ridge tops the scree slope rising directly above the west side. Huge chunks of gnarled driftwood punctuate meadows and wide beaches along the eastern shore. This is a prime place to explore and take a break for lunch.

Cross a low saddle at the south end of the lake and wind down a rocky hill on a faint path curving east to Smoky Lake. This emerald green gem lies in a rocky bowl backed by wooded ridges. Skirt the northeast shore and follow an overgrown path down the north side of the outlet through clusters of shooting stars and monkeyflowers.

Contour eastward down the widening canyon, staying high to avoid a tangle

# HIKE 37b  *Norton Lakes Loop*

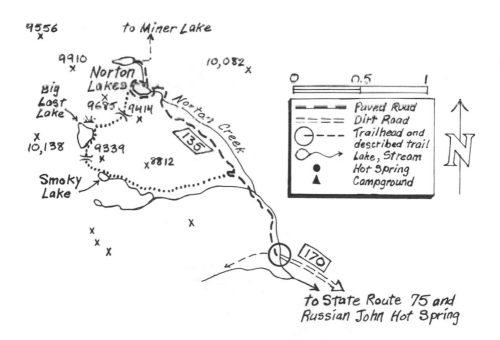

*Driftwood logs hug the outlet of Lower Norton Lake—the first stop on the Norton Lakes Loop.*

of downed trees below. Continue about 1.5 miles below Smoky Lake to intersect Norton Lake Trail in a forested area. Not to worry—you can't miss it. Follow the trail back down the hill for the last mile.

# 38 Elkhorn Hot Spring

**General description:** A riverside hot box below a highway, near Stanley and the eastern Sawtooth trailheads, in the SNRA. Swimwear essential. Elevation 6,100 feet.

**Directions:** Drive two miles east of Lower Stanley on State Route 75. Watch for a small pullout by the river in the middle of a curve 0.7 mile east of milepost 192 (local folks call the spot First Bend Hot Spring). Park here and climb down the rocks. Elkhorn isn't marked on the forest map.

**The hot spring:** This is the first of several hot dips along the Salmon River Scenic Route east of Stanley. A few shallow pools and a one-body soaking box tucked between boulders mark the highly visible spot. Scalding hot, 136-degree water is piped under the highway to the tub, and the only way to cool it is to scramble back and forth over the rocks to the river with a bucket. If somebody has made off with the bucket, you're out of luck!

*Locals call this tub at Elkhorn Hot Spring the "boat box" because of it popularity with kayakers and commercial raft groups.*

# HIKE 38a  *Alpine, Sawtooth, and McGown Lakes*

**General description:** A moderate 12-mile, round-trip day hike or overnighter featuring alpine views and the largest lake in the Sawtooth Wilderness, near Elkhorn Hot Spring.
**Elevation gain and loss:** +2,090 feet, -280 feet.
**Trailhead elevation:** 6,710 feet.
**High point:** 8,800 feet.
**Maps:** Stanley Lake 7.5-minute USGS quad; Sawtooth National Forest.

**Finding the trailhead:** Drive 2.5 miles west of Stanley on State Route 21. Turn left onto gravel Iron Creek Road (Forest Road 619) and drive three miles to a campground loop at the road's end. The trailhead for these lakes as well as Goat Lake is located near the far end of the loop.

**The hike:** The star attraction of this highly popular trip is the giant sapphire oval of Sawtooth Lake. Craggy Mt. Regan dominates the skyline directly across the granite bowl, and trails around both sides offer a variety of unobstructed views. This may well be the most shutterbugged scene in the Sawtooths; it's a hard one to beat!

The Iron Creek Trail (640) meanders southwest for the first 1.25 miles to the wilderness line, then crosses Alpine Way branching east to Goat Lake (Hike 38b). The route curves gently to a second junction in a boggy flat, then angles up an open slope above Iron Creek valley.

Splash across Iron Creek and climb to an overlook of Alpine Lake in four miles. A spur quickly drops to the north shore of this popular, emerald green gem fringed with subalpine fir, and Alpine Peak stands out to the south above the treetops.

The main trail snakes west above Alpine Lake. The ridgetop has views of peaks to the north and south and overlooks the Iron Creek valley stretching east toward Stanley. A bit more scenic climbing brings you past a small tarn in an alpine valley to the outlet and northern end of the largest lake in the Sawtooths at five miles, 8,430 feet.

Starkly beautiful Sawtooth Lake stretches a full mile from head to toe and a half mile across. A deep basin of granite slabs outlines the oval shape, and a few twisted trees cling for survival to the steep walls. The jagged contours of Mt. Regan shoot 1,760 feet skyward from the surface at the far end.

There is a junction by the outlet. Before going on to McGown Lakes, take the left fork a short way south to a granite knoll with a full view across the lake. The scenic side path hugs the east shore for an easygoing mile to a flower-lined pond directly beneath Mt. Regan before dropping through a glacier-cut gap to reach Baron Creek Trail in six lightly traveled miles (see Hike 30b).

The main trail branches west to climb 360 feet in a .5-mile traverse across the steep north wall. This eye-catching stretch offers an eagle's perspective across the full length of the lake to Mt. Regan and the gap carved in the far wall. The path crests at 8,800 feet, the high point on the hike, then quickly drops into a rocky valley to reach the largest McGown Lake just south of the trail at six miles.

The McGown Lakes lie in shallow rock basins below low peaks. They haven't much to offer other than a couple of campsites, a few stunted trees, and the magnificent route connecting them with Sawtooth Lake a mile away.

*Looking down the length of mile-long Sawtooth Lake, craggy Mt. Regan dominates the southern horizon.*

# HIKE 38b  *Goat Lake*

**General description:** A difficult 7-mile, round-trip day climb or overnighter (for mountain goats only) to a rock-walled lake in the Sawtooth Wilderness, near Elkhorn Hot Spring.
**Elevation gain and loss:** +1,750 feet, -240 feet.
**Trailhead elevation:** 6,710 feet.
**High point:** Goat Lake, 8,220 feet.
**Maps:** Same as Hike 38a.

**Finding the trailhead:** Follow the road access for Hike 38a.

**The hike:** A second trek from the Iron Creek Trailhead offers a challenging route to a lake hemmed in by sheer granite cliffs. Hanging snowfields on the far wall cast chunks of ice into the water. A misty waterfall threads its way down from two higher lakes, and another cascade borders the climb in. The trip isn't recommended for young children or inexperienced hikers, as much of the route is a steep scramble on loose rock. Good hiking boots are a must.

Follow Iron Creek Trail (640) 1.25 miles southwest through a lodgepole pine forest, past the wilderness boundary, to a trail junction in a grassy valley. The right fork continues up Iron Creek valley to Alpine, Sawtooth, and McGown Lakes (Hike 38a); the left fork is signed "to Marshall Lake" and traces the wilderness line southeast.

Turn east onto Alpine Way (528) and cross Iron Creek on a shaky (if still standing) footbridge. Pass through a boggy forest, then wade a small stream laced with wildflowers where the trail contours north around a wooded ridge. It swings slowly southward and then veers sharply northeast a second time at 2.75 miles.

Leave the main trail behind here and turn right on a primitive path climbing southwest below a cliff. A spur branches downhill in .25 mile to the base of Goat Creek Falls for a squint at the misty cascade. The track to the lake becomes increasingly eroded and slippery. Look south at the first switchback to another ribbon of falls across the basin; farther south, Williams and Thompson Peaks slice into the ragged horizon. The path shoots up the north canyon wall to the top of the falls, gaining 800 feet in the .75-mile climb from Alpine Way.

Cross the creek above the falls on a handy log, then hike the last hundred yards to reach the north shore of Goat Lake at 3.5 miles. Cliffs on three sides rise 1,500 feet above the surface, and jagged towers lean out as if ready to leap. Experts can boulder-hop around the east shore to compare views, but the traverse is steep and tricky.

*"The Leaning Latrine":* *Iron Creek Campground, at the time I was there, had an unusual feature—an outhouse tipped forward on a slant. I was unaware of this as I approached one night without a flashlight. The door seemed hard to open, and then it slammed shut behind me! In total darkness, I found myself staggering to stand upright and reach the seat. I couldn't understand what was wrong—I'd only had one beer after the hike. The following morning it all became clear when I saw that it was the outhouse, and not me, that was tipsy.*

*A jumbled mass of ridges and peaks, seen from the log jam at the outlet, walls in the south shore of Goat Lake.*

# HIKE 38a  *Alpine, Sawtooth, and McGown Lakes*
# HIKE 38b  *Goat Lake*

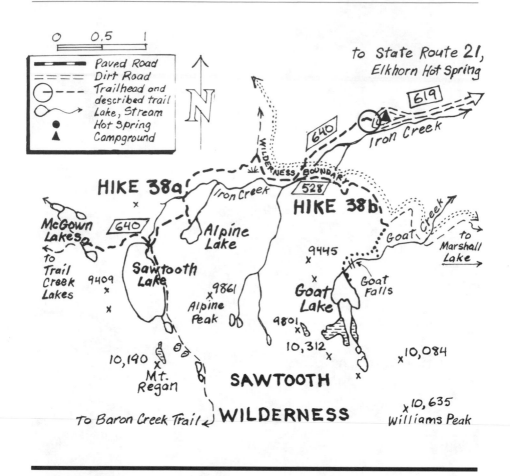

**Map legend:**
Paved Road
Dirt Road
Trailhead and described trail
Lake, Stream
Hot Spring
Campground

# HIKE 38c  *Cramer Lakes*

**General description:** A moderate 14.5-mile, round-trip backpack up a glacial canyon leading to high lakes, wildflowers, and breathtaking views in the Sawtooth Wilderness, near Elkhorn Hot Spring.
**Elevation gain and loss:** 1,840 feet.
**Trailhead elevation:** 6,560 feet.
**High point:** Upper Cramer Lake, 8,400 feet.
**Maps:** Mt. Cramer and Warbonnet Peak 7.5-minute USGS quads; Sawtooth National Forest.

**Finding the trailhead:** Drive 4.5 miles south of Stanley on State Route 75 and turn right on Redfish Lake Road. Drive two miles to a sign on the right marking the backpacker's parking lot. This is the only spot you can leave your car for overnight trips.

**The hike:** A boot-beaten path up a deep canyon bordered by the best known and most climbed peaks in the Sawtooths branches south to the Cramer Lakes in a popular hike from Redfish Lake. Inviting campsites at Middle Cramer face a waterfall across the blue-green water. Upper Cramer, the largest of the three, sits directly beneath the towering face of a 10,500-foot peak. Mt. Cramer peeks from behind the canyon leading south to Cramer Divide.

With the help of the Redfish Lake ferry, you can save 5.5 miles of walking to the far end. The scenic 20-minute ride offers face-on views of Mt. Heyburn's sheer cliffs and the sharp pinnacles of The Grand Mogul guarding the head of the lake. The ferry drops hikers at Redfish Lake Inlet Transfer Camp. Trail mileage and elevation gain are given from this point.

Redfish Lake Creek Trail (101) starts west above the developed inlet campground in heavy timber and climbs alongside the rushing creek into the wide, U-shaped canyon. Pop out of the woods at the base of Mt. Heyburn and zigzag past a junction with the lakeside trail. Continue southwest with a moderate climb past a stretch where house-sized boulders almost block the path. Climbers enjoy this area for its solid rock and easy access.

The path continues southwest alongside the plunging creek and passes occasional waterfalls, then climbs through a forest of lodgepole pines, spruce, and fir with frequent glimpses of the spires and domes rimming the canyon walls. You'll pass the orange-hued Saddleback at two miles, nicknamed by climbers the Elephant's Perch. Continue past Goat and Eagle Perches to reach Flatrock Junction at 3.5 miles, 7,400 feet.

At Flatrock Junction, named for the granite slabs filling the canyon floor, the trail splits. The right fork branches off to cross Baron Divide, drop to Baron Lakes and finally exit at Grandjean in a total of 18.5 miles (see Hike 30b). The left fork climbs past the Cramer Lakes over 9,480 foot Cramer Divide, and offers access to many classic lakes and peaks farther south.

Turn south onto Cramer Lakes Trail (154). You can ford Redfish Lake Creek on a log jam downstream or wade across on slabs 200 yards above. Stroll .5 mile upstream through forest, then follow switchbacks up the canyon wall to a hanging valley where the route swings southeast. Enjoy views across to craggy Reward and Elk Peaks. A last gentle stretch brings you to Lower Cramer Lake at 6.8 miles. Settle down here for a bit of solitude, or walk another .5 mile to the upper lakes for less privacy but wall-to-wall views.

The graceful 20-foot waterfall at Middle Cramer Lake makes an idyllic setting for the large campsite facing it at the outlet, while tiny tentsites along the narrow shelf between the upper two lakes combine a vertical view down the broad falls with a panorama of jagged peaks rimming Upper Cramer Lake. It's a delightfully difficult choice!

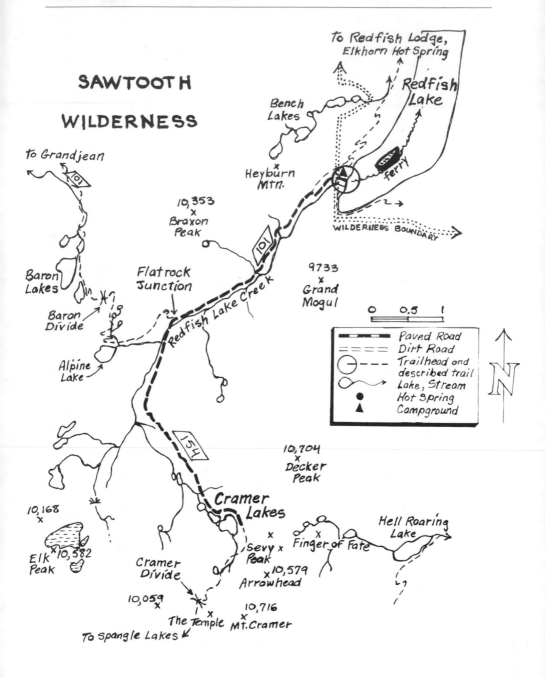

SAWTOOTH

WILDERNESS

To Grandjean

To Redfish Lodge,
Elkhorn Hot Spring

Redfish
Lake

Bench
Lakes

Heyburn
x
Mtn.

Ferry

10,353
x
Braxon
Peak

WILDERNESS BOUNDARY

Flatrock
Junction

9733
x
Grand
Mogul

Baron
Lakes

Baron
Divide

Redfish Lake Creek

0      0.5      1

Alpine
Lake

Paved Road
Dirt Road
Trailhead and
described trail
Lake, Stream
Hot Spring
Campground

N

154

10,704
x
Decker
Peak

Cramer
Lakes

10,168
x

Hell Roaring
Lake

Elk
Peak
x 10,582

Cramer
Divide

x
Sevy  x
Peak

x
Finger of Fate

x 10,579
Arrowhead

10,059
x

10,716
x
Mt. Cramer

The Temple

To Spangle Lakes

# 39 Campground Hot Spring

**General description:** Soaking pools hiding out in a campground, near Stanley and the eastern Sawtooth trailheads, in the SNRA. Daytime skinnydipping not recommended. Elevation 6,100 feet.

**Directions:** Drive seven miles east of Stanley on State Route 75 to Basin Creek Campground. Pull into campsite four and wander casually into the bushes. You'll have to wade the small creek to reach the pools. The riverside dips across the highway (see below) are larger but more heavily used. The spring isn't marked on the forest map.

**The hot spring:** What most folks stopping here never discover is that there happens to be a small hot spring on the creek flowing past the campsites; the bushy border screens a couple of pleasant soaking pools from view. The temperature can be controlled by adjusting the creekside rocks. A semi-private spot in a public campground!

**HOT SPRING 38** *Elkhorn Hot Spring*
**HOT SPRING 39** *Campground Hot Spring*
**HOT SPRING 40** *Basin Creek Hot Spring*
**HOT SPRING 41** *Sunbeam Hot Springs*

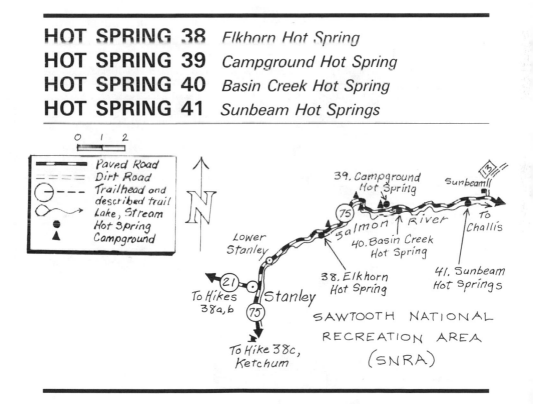

# 40 Basin Creek Hot Spring

**General description:** Hot dips sandwiched between the highway and the Salmon River, near Stanley and the eastern Sawtooth trailheads, in the SNRA. Swimwear advised. Elevation 6,100 feet.

**Directions:** Drive seven miles east of Stanley on State Route 75. Just beyond Basin Creek Campground (see above), turn right onto a short spur that dead-ends at the soaking pools and an unofficial camping area by the river. The spring isn't shown on the forest map.

**The hot spring:** This semi-secluded spot, also known as Kem Hot Spring, may be the best of several roadside dips along the Salmon River Scenic Route east of Stanley. It's located at the base of a bank below the busy highway; motorists speeding by wouldn't be too likely to notice a few bathers unless they knew just where to look.

Two family-sized soakers (often filled to capacity) border the river. Rocks enclosing them can be moved to either divert the 137-degree spring water or admit cold river water. The pools swamp during high water and the rocks wash away; they often take on a new look every summer depending on the talents of the volunteers who rebuild them.

*The pools at Basin Creek Hot Spring lie at the river's edge and must be rebuilt every year when the water level drops.*

# 41 Sunbeam Hot Springs

**General description:** Highly visible pools and a tub, squeezed between the highway and the Salmon River, east of Stanley in the SNRA. No nudes, just prunes and prudes. Elevation 6,100 feet.

**Directions:** Drive about 11 miles east of Stanley on State Route 75 (four miles past Basin Creek Hot Spring or a mile west of Sunbeam Resort). Look for a boarded-up stone bathhouse in a large turnout. A short path leads from the west end to the pools, and a path at the east end drops down to the soaking box. The springs are named on the forest map.

**The hot springs:** One last cluster of highway hot soaks lines the Salmon River Scenic Route from Stanley to Challis. Boiling water flows across a gravel beach into several popular pools at the river's edge. Bathers can adjust the rocks to create a variety of soaking temperatures.

A few hundred feet downstream, a handcrafted wooden tub is embedded in the rocks above the river. A length of hose feeds steamy water into the one-body box, and a handy bucket (usually) sits around to add river water with. Without the mix, the temperature's too hot for soaking, so let's hope the bucket is still there!

*With a few buckets of river water tossed in, this soaking box at Sunbeam can be quite enjoyable. The stone building above it was built in the 1930s as a public bathhouse.*

# 42 Upper Loon Creek Hot Springs

## HIKE 42a *To Upper Loon Creek Hot Springs*

**General description:** An easy 11.5-mile, round-trip day hike or overnighter to a chain of pearls lost on a creek above the Middle Fork Salmon River, northeast of Stanley in the River of No Return Wilderness. A skinnydipper's delight.
**Elevation gain and loss:** +240 feet, -640 feet.
**High point:** Trailhead, 5,400 feet.
**Low point:** Owen cabin, 5,040 feet.
**Maps:** River of No Return Wilderness, South half (Forest Service contour map) or Castro, Falconberry Peak, and Rock Creek 7.5-minute USGS quads; Challis National Forest.

**Finding the trailhead:** Drive about 12 miles east of Stanley on State Route 75 (a mile past Sunbeam Hot Springs) to Sunbeam Resort. Turn left on the Yankee Fork Road (Forest Road 13) and drive eight easy miles north to Bonanza, home of the historic Yankee Fork Dredge that sits marooned in a small pond walled in by the rocks it dredged out of the creek.

Bear left beyond the barge onto rocky Loon Creek Road (172) which follows Jordan Creek north past other historic sites to Loon Creek summit. The seasonal road (July 1 to November 1) snakes over the 8,700-foot crest that forms the wilderness boundary and down the far side to eventually reach the road-

*This 5-star, crescent-shaped pool at Upper Loon Creek Hot Springs was built right under a hot waterfall.*

end trailhead in a total of 33 dusty miles. Tin Cup Campground, a mile from the end, provides a welcome rest. The springs are marked on the forest maps.

**The hike:** Five wilderness hot springs lie at close intervals on Upper Loon Creek in the Salmon River Mountains north of Sunbeam. All five are located on the east (trail) side of the broad creek, and all branch into steamy channels that either trickle or tumble down the rocky banks. They vary in appearance from interesting to spectacular and in usability from "for display purposes only" to outstanding.

Loon Creek Trail (101), a pleasant stroll, is far less tiring than the access road. The canyon walls are coated with grass and sagebrush on the south-facing slopes while the hills facing north are lightly wooded with Douglas-fir. The upper canyon consists of talus slopes and rock outcrops patched with lime-yellow and orange lichen. Beyond an 800-foot face, the path fords small streams fringed by grassy flats. The route closely follows the lively creek, and in August and September you can sometimes see salmon struggling up the rapids to reach their spawning grounds.

The trail bridges Loon Creek at three miles, passes a few campsites, and soon reaches a stretch of midsummer berry picking interspersed with more easy stream hopping. At five miles are the remains of a log cabin (still in one piece) hidden in a tangle of greenery down by the creek. The first hot spring branches into a broad flow over the rocky flat, and a few shallow pools edge the creek. There's a shaded campsite in the grass beside the cabin.

Just around the next bend, hot waterfalls from the two largest springs plunge over 20-foot cliffs into Loon Creek. A totally outstanding pool in the shape

## HIKE 42a  *To Upper Loon Creek Hot Springs*

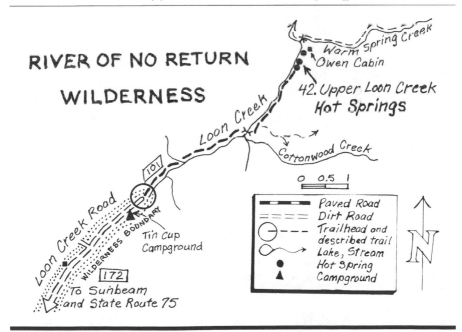

149

of a crescent has been built against the cliff directly below one of the falls. Green moss and ferns hug the bank beneath the misty spray. The temperature may be a smidge too hot, but the rocks lining the bubbly can be rearranged to admit a cold mix from the creek. The outflow swirls with a delicious marbling of hot and cold currents into a protected alcove alongside.

The last two hot springs emerge in a meadow a scant .5 mile farther on. They flow gently through the grass into pools of rust-colored algae, then continue down the bank to fill shallow, rock-lined pools by the creek. The crumbling ruins of the historic Owen cabin, engulfed in vegetation, lie just beyond the wide meadow. From this point, one could take Warm Spring Creek Trail 8.5 miles upstream, fording it six times and passing more hot springs at Foster Ranch, as an alternate route to Shower Bath Hot Springs (see Hike 44a).

# 43 Slate Creek Hot Spring

**General description:** A rustic bathhouse in a wooded canyon near a dirt road, southeast of Stanley in the SNRA. Wear what you bathe in at home. Elevation 7,040 feet.

**Directions:** Drive about 23 miles east of Stanley on State Route 75. Turn right on Slate Creek Road (Forest Road 666) just beyond a bridge over the Salmon River. Drive seven bumpy miles south to a roadblock, climb the gate, and walk a few hundred yards up the road. The spring is named on the forest map.

**The hot spring:** A funky but functional bathhouse straddles a hot spring (also known as "Hoodoo") on the wooded bank above a creek. An incoming hose feeds 122-degree water into a recessed, soaker-friendly box big enough to hold two cozy bodies, and a second hose admits cold water. A removable slat in the wall lets the water drain out. The system works great!

The crude structure was pieced together from whatever materials came to hand. The walls are a mixture of logs, planks, and plywood. The roof is open to the elements at the end above the soaking box, and a hole for a window lets the bather enjoy the view downhill. An old red blanket hanging on a nail can be hooked over the doorway to let visitors know when the tub is in use.

# HIKE 43a  *Crater Lake*

**General description:** A moderate 8-mile, round-trip day hike or overnighter to a quiet lake in the White Cloud Mountains, near Slate Creek Hot Spring.
**Elevation gain and loss:** 2,480 feet.
**Trailhead elevation:** 6,440 feet.
**High point:** Crater Lake, 8,920 feet.
**Maps:** Livingston Creek 7.5-minute USGS quad; Sawtooth National Forest.

**Finding the trailhead:** Follow the directions above to Slate Creek Road and

# HOT SPRING 43  *Slate Creek Hot Spring*
# HIKE 43a  *Crater Lake*

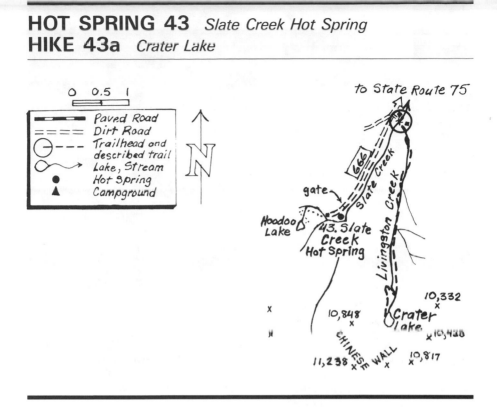

drive upcanyon 5.6 miles. Turn left at the second ranch to the road-end parking area at Slate Creek. The trail is shown on the forest map but not on the USGS quad.

**The hike:** A pleasant walk up a lively creek reaches grey-blue Crater Lake tucked between twisted ridges in a lightly used part of the Sawtooth National Recreation Area. The route has many stream fords but is easy to follow. Hoodoo Lake, the only other hike near Slate Creek Hot Spring, is a tough scramble up a hill riddled with eroded mining roads. Of the two, Crater Lake is much easier to find, has a better track to hike, and offers closer views of the surrounding peaks in the White Clouds.

Cross the creek on a footbridge and walk an abandoned mining road that's been blocked to motor vehicles with strategically placed piles of rock. The route follows Livingston Creek due south for four miles to the lake. At most of the stream crossings, you'll find handy rocks or logs to balance your way across on.

The route for the first mile or so is a fairly gentle climb through deep woods, then it begins to steepen. At three miles, there's an open traverse with increasingly broad views as the track heads up the rocky canyon wall. Make one giant switchback at the head of the canyon to reach the outlet of Crater Lake at four miles.

Wander around the lake on either side and enjoy views of the contorted

*You can't judge a book by its cover. The shack at Slate Creek Hot Spring has a way of eliciting smiles of contentment from those who venture within its patchwork walls.*

Chinese Wall—a striated ridge that buckles in the center as if someone had tried to lift it off the ground from both ends! Across from the Chinese Wall is the rounded end of Railroad Ridge. A sawtoothed crest fills the gap in between. The unusual basin gives a touch of class to an otherwise modest lake.

*"Pain remedy": Halfway through a peanut butter and carrot sandwich, as I sat on a warm rock gazing up at the Chinese Wall, the sky suddenly turned darker than Slate Creek below. I'd just gulped down the last bite when the drops started to fall, and the drizzle turned to a spitting downpour before I was halfway down the trail. The harder it poured, the faster I ran!*

*I'd no sooner leaped into the car when the sky turned a sickly shade of yellow and let loose a wild volley of hailstones. The ground, covered with dancing snow peas, turned white in an instant. I slithered the last mile up the road with a smile on my face because the perfect antidote to nasty weather was close at hand. Ten minutes later, I slid into a cocoon of steamy water and leaned back against a handy plank. Sleet and hail pelted the crude shelter at Slate Creek Hot Spring while I waited out the storm in total comfort.*

# G. OUT OF CHALLIS

A hair-raising but spectacular drive northwest of Challis climbs a convoluted crest deep into the River of No Return Wilderness. At 29 miles, a path plunges down to a five-star soak at Shower Bath (Hike 44a); at the road end, a long descent to the Middle Fork Salmon River ends up at two more wilderness gems (Hike 45/46a). And back on US 93 north of Challis, a last walk leads to Goldbug's hot bubblies cascading through a desert canyon (Hike 47a).

# 44 Shower Bath Hot Springs

## HIKE 44a *To Shower Bath Hot Springs*

**General description:** A grueling 12-mile, round-trip day hike or overnighter to a geothermal fairyland on a remote creek above the Middle Fork, northwest of Challis in the River of No Return Wilderness. Swimwear superfluous baggage.
**Elevation gain and loss:** +100 feet, -2,340 feet.
**High point:** Trailhead, 8,040 feet.
**Low point:** Shower Bath, 5,800 feet.
**Maps:** Sheldon Peak 7.5-minute USGS quad or River of No Return Wilderness, South half (Forest Service contour map); Challis National Forest.

**The vision and the challenge:** Imagine stumbling knee deep in a torrent of icy water through a deep chasm that sees maybe an hour of sun a day, rounding the last bend numb and exhausted, and finding paradise spread out before you. Steamy water flows over the sides of a wide alcove and splashes into rocky bowls below. Clouds of spray billow out over a soft green carpet beyond the pools. Peering through the mist, you can almost conjure up a row of angels drying their wings in the sun after a heavenly soak.

But, like the legendary Shangri-la, Shower Bath lies at the end of an exhausting and difficult trek. Some 29 teeth-jarring miles on a knife-edged road are followed by a trail diving downhill into a stream that must be waded through a narrow gorge. The portal to paradise is the gorge, and the key to unlock it is proper timing. The last 300-yard stretch can be waist deep through late July; when it is, Warm Spring Creek can't be waded with any degree of safety. Be sure to check with the Forest Service in Challis before attempting the trip.

**Finding the trailhead:** The odyssey begins by taking U.S. Highway 93 to Challis. Turn right at McPherson's store and drive nine paved miles north and west into Challis National Forest-where pavement ends and Sleeping Deer Road (Forest Road 86) begins. Bear right at 10.5 miles and right again at a confusing junction at 15 miles. Climb a very rocky surface to crest at 10,334 feet on Twin Peaks (the wilderness boundary). The seasonal road (August 1 to October 1) irons out somewhat beyond the top but becomes very narrow; sheer dropoffs are offset by wall-to-wall views.

Shortly past a turnoff to Mahoney Springs Camp at about 28 miles, you'll see the first of two signs a mile apart that both read "to Warm Spring Creek Trail". The first claims five miles; the second (located opposite the Fly Creek trailhead) states seven. With all due respect to the Forest Service, it seems they were planted in reverse order—the second is the shorter route. Shower Bath is named on all three maps. See the following hike for another adventure at the end of the road and Hike 42a for an alternate route to Shower Bath by way of Upper Loon Creek Hot Springs.

**The hike:** Drop over the edge on a path that plunges 760 feet in the first mile

*The persevering hiker will find one or more rocky soaking pools at Shower Bath Hot Springs hidden behind a curtain of steam and fine spray.*

to reach a spring, two old log huts, and a junction where the two trails join together to follow Mahoney Creek downhill. The grueling route dives another mile through heavy timber to a side stream, after which the grade becomes more moderate.

The sinuous track weaves across Mahoney Creek wherever the canyon walls get too snug on one side. When you're not fording the main creek, you'll be jumping the many side streams that feed it. Continue down through a colorful blend of pine, fir, and aspen to finally bottom out on a sagebrush flat at Warm Spring Creek with a total loss of 2,340 feet in five miles.

Take a breather and stroll upstream on Warm Spring Creek Trail past the old Warm Spring Ranger Cabin (built in 1910) and on to the mouth of the narrows. Prepare for a cold plunge as rock walls 200 feet high funnel the path into the swift moving creek. Work your way upstream taking care to avoid the deeper holes. The path emerges briefly along the west bank, then drops back into the stream. Tiny hot springs trickle down the sheer walls, but these

# HIKE 44a  *To Shower Bath Hot Springs*

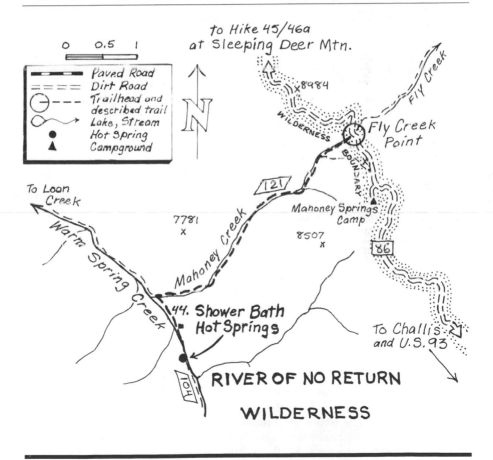

aren't the ones you came this far to see. Round the final bend and haul out on dry land on the west bank at six miles.

Shower Bath is the ultimate experience in wilderness hot springs—guaranteed to meet your wildest dreams! A broad wall of water trickles and tumbles in a 40-foot drop over the rim, and rainbows shimmer overhead as sunlight pours through the mist. Gushing from the ground above at 120 degrees, the flow cools to a perfect soak in the tiny soaking pools directly below.

Colorful lichen speckles the rock-ribbed walls, and moisture-loving grasses carpet the floor with inviting campsites. A warm stream meanders through the meadow to another soaking pool spread out by the creek. Enjoy your stay, but please treat the fragile ecosystem around the springs with the respect it deserves.

# 45/46 Lower Loon Creek & Cox Hot Springs

## HIKE 45/46a  *To Both Hot Springs*

**General description:** A rugged 35-mile, round-trip backpack featuring hot dips in the Middle Fork Salmon River Canyon, northwest of Challis in the depths of the River of No Return Wilderness. "Prudes out, nudes in" is the Middle Fork motto.
**Elevation gain and loss:** +120 feet, -5,420 feet.
**High point:** Trailhead, 9,340 feet.
**Low point:** Lower Loon Creek, 4,040 feet.
**Maps:** Sleeping Deer Mtn. and Ramey Hill 7.5-minute USGS quads or River of No Return Wilderness, South half (Forest Service contour map); Challis National Forest.

**Finding the trailhead:** Follow the spine-tingling access road described in Hike 44a above. Continue along the narrow crest to reach the road-end trail sign in about 43 total miles. Perch your car in the tiny pullout and dig out your dusty boots. Lower Loon Creek Hot Springs is marked without a name on the USGS quad; Cox is named on all three maps.

**The hike:** A long and lonesome journey offers the more adventurous hiker a chance to sample a broad cross section of the River of No Return Wilderness as well as a steamy double dip at the rainbow's end. The path begins in subalpine forest on a frosty mountaintop. Two life zones, 14 miles, and well over 5,000 feet below, it comes to rest in the semi-arid canyon carved by the Middle Fork Salmon River. Sagebrush lines the way to Cox Hot Springs, and a twilight forest of ponderosa pine frames the stroll up Loon Creek to one of the finest hot pools in the wilderness.

High lakes below the trailhead draw an occasional fisherman, and the distant hot springs attract seasonal boatloads of river rats, but the rugged backcountry here sees almost no visitors at all. Pristine scenery and solitude more than make up for the roundabout route.

Martin Mountain Trail (103) spends the first mile contouring around a knoll studded with whitebark pine to a 3-way junction on a high saddle. The left fork drops to Cabin Creek while the middle path climbs a mile to the lookout cabin on the 9,881-foot summit of Sleeping Deer Mountain. The right fork takes you down a precipitous slope, where it then traverses beneath the lookout to reach another saddle 200 feet below the first. This stretch is usually snow covered until mid-July. The path is hard to trace across the second rocky saddle.

The route drops northward between granite slabs to a long meadow at the head of Cache Creek. Five glacially-carved lakes fan out at half-mile intervals. You'll pass the first lake in the marshy meadow and see a log cabin nearby that's used by outfitters during the hunting season. Good campsites are located at the head of the lake and beside the cabin, elevation 8,685 feet.

*The soaking pool at Lower Loon Creek Hot Springs, visited chiefly by river rafting groups, has all the key ingredients to keep a boater or backpacker happy for hours.*

The trail contours an open ridge that overlooks Cache Creek Canyon and the second lake bordered by grassy meadows. As it swings around the head-wall, there are views of other lakes and the rugged Salmon River Mountains below. You'll reach a signed junction at about 4 miles. The right fork branches off to Woodtick Summit and continues on to Martin Mountain.

Turn left and zigzag down a grassy slope on the Woodtick Cutoff Trail past a small lake on your left to reach a branch of Cache Creek 400 feet below. Ford the creek to meet the rugged trail you'll be following down to the river. This 10-mile stretch offers few level campsites and difficult access to water, so it might be best to spend the first night somewhere around the lakes.

Cache Creek Trail (100) dives down the headwall of the craggy canyon. The route passes primeval forests and lush meadows, and at times you'll hear the roar of Cache Creek far below. As you continue the grueling plunge, deep forests are gradually left behind. Grass and sagebrush begin to speckle the dry south-facing slopes, and the cooler hills facing north become wooded with stocky pines.

Finally, near the bottom, come two sets of stream crossings where you can count on wet feet. Shortly beyond the last ford, the trail comes to rest at a junction. Bear left on the Middle Fork Trail to Loon Creek Pack Bridge, at 4,030 feet-14 miles and 5,300 feet below the trailhead on Sleeping Deer Mountain. Turn left across the bridge to find Lower Loon Creek Hot Springs .25 mile upstream.

You'll discover a rectangular pool lined with split logs—at least 20 feet long, 10 feet across, and three or four feet deep. Fed by several springs with temperatures up to 120 degrees, the flow cools to a blissful soak en route through a long hose to the crystal-clear pool. One side is shaded by a canopy of evergreen boughs while a few planks on the creek side form a spacious sun deck. The setting is a fine blend of seclusion and open views.

For the 7-mile round trip from here to Cox, head .5 mile downstream to the river and swing west up the Middle Fork Trail. The gentle route passes sagebrush slopes dotted with age-old ponderosas. You'll spot Cox Campground down on a sand bar dominated by one tall pine three miles upstream. The springs are located on the second bench above it, at 4160 feet. The lower bench holds a tadpole-laden pond and the grave of Whitey Cox—a miner who died in a rockslide in 1954 while prospecting the area.

The few shallow soaking pools here lie out in a meadow strewn with wildflowers. There isn't much flow-through by late summer from the 130-degree springs, and the silty bottoms stir up easily. The pools don't have much to offer the gourmet hot springer other than countless acres of solitude, a pleasant view across the canyon, and the highly scenic 3-mile stroll along a wild and grand old river.

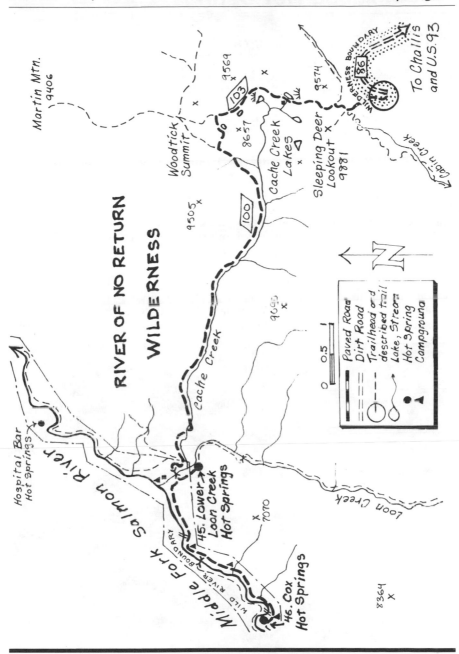

# 47 Goldbug Hot Springs

## HIKE 47a *To Goldbug Hot Springs*

**General description:** A moderate 4-mile, round-trip day climb to steamy soaks and waterfalls in a desert canyon, between Challis and Salmon. Keep a swimsuit handy.
**Elevation gain and loss:** +920 feet, -120 feet.
**Trailhead elevation:** 4,400 feet.
**High point:** Goldbug, 5,200 feet.
**Maps:** Goldbug Ridge 7.5-minute USGS quad; Salmon National Forest.

**Finding the trailhead:** Drive about 35 miles north of Challis or 23 miles south of Salmon on U.S. Highway 93. Near milepost 282, turn east on a short gravel road ending at the trailhead parking area. Most of the 2-mile trail is on Bureau of Land Management Land, but the springs are in Salmon National Forest. Neither Goldbug nor the trail are marked on the maps.

**The hike:** One final gem winds up the tour of Idaho's natural hot springs. A brisk climb up a craggy desert canyon ends at a green oasis where lush undergrowth borders a tumbling stream. Hot and cold springs mix underground here and emerge as warm geothermal cascades that flow over dropoffs

*The large "rollercoaster" pool at Goldbug features a bizarre water slide that tumbles down from upper pools, then bounces up and billows out over the surface.*

down the rocky floor. A chain of bubbly pools of varying temperatures punctuates the space between falls.

A trailhead bridge spans Warm Spring Creek, and four switchbacks drag the new trail 200 feet uphill on the south side. The route turns east to traverse an open slope, then soon drops down to cross a second bridge. Greedy cottonwoods and willows choke the creek in a green line winding up the valley between dry sagebrush slopes dotted with pinyon and juniper. Ahead, Goldbug Ridge reveals a jagged slit.

The path crosses a third bridge near the canyon's mouth, then zigzags up the south wall passing several warm to hot soaking pools and falls on the way up. To find more bubblies, cross the fourth bridge and drop a short distance down the north wall. Moisture-loving greenery hugs the banks and overhangs the stream to create a private world around each sparkling pool.

## HIKE 47a  *To Goldbug Hot Springs*

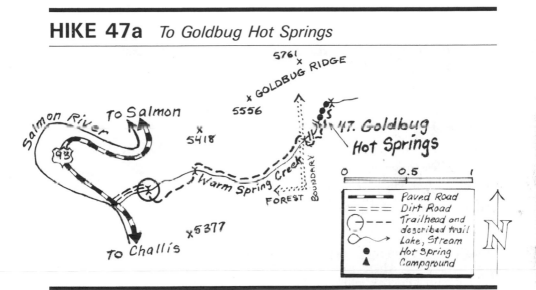

## FOR MORE INFORMATION

Contact the following Forest Service district offices for current conditions of hiking trails, stream crossings, and access roads. Forest and wilderness maps may be purchased at any district office or from offices of adjoining national forests.

**Hikes 11a,b:** Lochsa Ranger Station, Clearwater National Forest, P.O. Box 398, Kooskia, ID 83539; 208/926-4275.

**Hikes 13a-c:** Powell District, Clearwater National Forest, Milepost 162, Highway 12 at Powell Junction, (mail): Lolo, MT 59847; 208/942-3113.

**Hikes 17a and 18a:** Cascade District, Boise National Forest, P.O. Box 696, Cascade, ID 83611; 208/382-4271.

**Hikes 19a,b:** Krassel District, Payette National Forest, P.O. Box 1026, McCall, ID 83638; 208/634-8151.

**Hike 20a:** Boise National Forest but administered by the Middle Fork District, Challis National Forest, P.O. Box 750, Challis, ID 83226; 208/879-5204.

**Hikes 24/25a and 26a,b:** Emmett District, Boise National Forest, 1648 North Washington, Emmett, ID 83617; 208/365-4382 (or check at the Garden Valley Ranger Station).

**Hikes 28a,b and 31a,b:** Lowman District, Boise National Forest, Lowman, ID 83637; 208/259-3361.

**Hikes 30a,b:** Administered by the Sawtooth NRA, Headquarters Office, Star Route (Highway 75), Ketchum, ID 83340; 208/726-8291. Or check at the ranger station in Stanley.

**Hike 32/33a:** Middle Fork District, Challis National Forest, P.O. Box 750, Challis, ID 83226; 208/879-5204 (or check at the Boundary Creek Guard Station).

**Hikes 35a-c:** Same as 30a,b

**Hikes 37a,b:** Ketchum District, Sawtooth National Forest, Sun Valley Rd., Ketchum, ID 83340; 208/622-5371.

**Hikes 38a-c and 43a:** Same as 30a,b

**Hike 42a:** Yankee Fork District, Challis National Forest, HC 63, Box 650, Clayton, ID 83227; 208/838-2201.

**Hike 44a:** Challis District, Challis National Forest, P.O. Box 337, Challis, ID 83226; 208/879-4321.

**Hike 45/46a:** Same as 32/33a.

**Hike 47a:** Salmon District, Salmon National Forest, P.O. Box 729, Salmon, ID 83467; 208/756-3724.

For the most up-to-date lowdown on hot springs of all types, throughout the west and elsewhere, refer to "The Hot Springs Gazette," a quarterly review published by Roger Phillips, 12 S. Benton Ave., Helena, MT 59601.